PRAISE FOR *WORK LIFE BALANCING*

"I desperately needed advice concerning a life that I felt was spinning out of control. I read your book and have found your insights to be groundbreaking. I can't wait to apply your tenants toward a better balanced life."

**—Dr. Tom Phalen, IP Litigation Specialist
Kaye Scholer Attorneys At Law**

"Send me another copy! I have given your excellent book to my boss and I need to get an additional copy for me, as I absolutely want to keep this book as one of the regular ones to which I refer from time to time."

**—Benoît Lambillotte, Director Small & Med. Business
IBM Belgium, Netherlands, & Luxembourg**

"A must read for anyone who wonders how to do it all while remaining sane."

—Dr. Keri Pearlson, Founding Partner, KP Partners

"I was amazed...Paul's book had an immediate impact on my life within the first week of reading! I highly recommend it to any business owner who faces the constant pressure to produce results."

—John Yates, President & CEO, The Yates Group

"New hires, new managers, and Next Geners will love it."

—Matthew Ivis, Government Programs Manager, IBM Canada

"Anyone who wants to be 'successful' at work, life, and love, has to read this."

—Dr. George Dempsey, author of *Rescue Your Marriage Now!*

ACCLAIM FOR DR. PAUL BAFFES

"Paul's class was fantastic. I'm proud to work at a company that makes this kind of experience available to me."
—Utz Brenner, Partnership Manager SW Europe, IBM Germany

"Listening to Paul is better than Red Bull! I always leave super motivated!" **—Heather Pacaro, HR Partner, IBM Top Talent**

"Phenomenal presentation! Our in-box has received glowing reviews."
—Janet Carter, Rocky Mountain Women's Networking Group

"Every manager would benefit from Paul's work-life balancing class. It should be a required experience."
—Charles Senabulya, Manager Software Sales, IBM UK & Ireland

"Anyone who aspires for more productivity needs to take this class."
—Harini Chittor, Executive, Healthcare Services, IBM India

"Your talk was perfect. I've gotten a ton of thank you notes…one person has hung your 5 principles on the wall of her cube!"
—Dr. Lillian Davis, SAC Talk Radio

"I used to wonder why I never had time to do the things I wanted to do. Thanks, Paul, for helping me take back control of managing my time."
—Tony Carrato, Executive IT Architect, IBM Australia

"I now look at the things in a completely different way, and find I have higher quality on my 'deliverables', both in work and life. No kidding!"
—Rossana Sanguineti, Development Manager, IBM Venezuela

"I'm sure I speak for many: you've helped me find answers. Thanks, so much!" **—Louise Novak, Austin Women's Day**

"Thank you for your coaching; it has truly changed my life."
—Jeff Berkowitz, Senior IT Architect, IBM USA

Work-Life Balancing

How to be <u>Wildly</u> Successful in Both...Really!

Second Edition

Paul Baffes, Ph.D.

Copyright © 2005, 2006 by Paul Baffes

Published by Dr. WorkLife

ISBN 1-59872-749-4

Printed in the United States of America

SPECIAL SALES

Dr. WorkLife books are available at special quantity discounts to use for sales promotions, employee premiums, or educational purposes. For more information, please see our web site at www.drworklife.com or write to Dr. WorkLife, 8127 Mesa Drive, Suite B206-262, Austin, Texas, 78759.

For Kathryn...and for everything we've built together.

Special offers for purchasers of this book

Free Book Club Discussions

Thinking of holding a book club discussion on work-life balance? Dr. Baffes can be available, for FREE, to participate in discussions of this book via teleconference. Please send email to contact@drworklife.com for details, and for information on how to obtain DISCOUNTS for your entire book club membership.

Free Work-Life Balance Coaching

*Dr. Baffes offers a FREE introductory coaching SESSION to qualifying individuals. This introductory session can be for you alone OR for you and your spouse! (note: Dr Baffes is the only one we know who offers **COUPLES** work-life balance coaching!) Please contact us at contact@drworklife.com for details.*

Contents

Acknowledgements

A book like this isn't something you write by yourself. You "write" it over a period of years, by living it out through trial and error, with great people at your side who are patient enough to stick with you until you get things right. My thanks first to my wonderful wife, for slogging through all the effort, and for being so brilliant at so many crucial times when I couldn't see what was right in front of my nose. Thanks also to my long-time mentor and friend, George Dempsey, for teaching me, and "un-teaching" me, so much. And this book would never have happened if Heather Jackson hadn't put the wild idea into my head that I might actually have something useful to offer to others about this topic. Finally, thanks to my parents who had the courage to go against the odds and against deep cultural convention to show that it really is possible to live an ideal if you simply believe in it strongly enough.

Paul Baffes

Preface

The big rock story...

One day, a hard charging business school class had a guest lecture from a time management consultant. As you can imagine, these students were all type-As ready to take on the world and do things beyond the accomplishments of mere mortals. The time management consultant began his talk by walking up to a podium which concealed some props. "I am here today to talk to you about time management" he told them "and I will be using some props to help make my points."

He began by taking a large mason jar out from behind the podium. "This mason jar represents your calendar" he began "and, like all calendars, we 'fill up our time' with things we want to schedule. I will use different props to fill this mason jar, thus 'filling up' the calendar."

He then proceeded to take out big rocks and put them into the mason jar. He put as many in as he could, shaking the jar so that the rocks would settle down as far as possible to the bottom. When he had put as many big rocks as possible into the jar, he then turned to the MBAs and said "OK...so...is the jar full?"

The students exchanged several "duh" glances and then one student raised a hand and said "um...yes, it's full."

"Nope" replied the consultant. "Not even close." He then proceeded to take out medium-sized rocks and place them into the mason jar, again jiggling the jar until he put as many medium-sized rocks as possible into the jar. "Full now?" he asked.

By now, of course, the students were beginning to get the drift. Someone shouted out from the back "no!"

"Right!" said the consultant, and then proceeded to pull out small rocks and shake them down into the jar. This continued with pebbles, then sand, and finally, water. Each time the shouts of "no, not full yet!" got louder and louder.

After the water was in the jar, the consultant said "OK, so now, the jar really is full. Now, who can tell me the moral of this story?"

With that there was a moment of silence, until one of the type-As in the front row raised a hand and said "I know! The moral is this: no matter how full you think your calendar is, in reality, there is always time to fit something more in to your day."

"No!" said the consultant. "The moral is this:

IF YOU DON'T PUT THE BIG ROCKS IN FIRST, YOU'LL NEVER GET THEM IN."

How to Read This Book

Each chapter of this book is organized in two sections. The first is a principle of work-life balancing, shown in italics at the top, then described just below the italics. Following that comes a series of stories aimed at bringing the principle to life with real examples.

The problem with "work-life balance" is that it is misnamed. There really is no such thing as work-life "balance."

For example, I could tell you all about my own particular circumstances and how I manage to keep my life balanced. I could describe in detail the tricks my wife and I have devised to handle the morning routine with two small children, one of whom is in grade school, the other who goes to a day care center across town. I could weave in how we manage to make time for ourselves once a week and how I take advantage of the fact that I work for an incredibly family-friendly company by using telecommuting to do everything from waiting around for the cable guy to writing this book. The problem is, most of this advice would be irrelevant to most of you. Worse, it turns out that most of what I do now was irrelevant even for me just two years ago, and will become irrelevant again by the time August rolls around and my second daughter enters kindergarten.

The issue here, of course, is that life isn't static. It's not the same for any two people. I have kids; some of you reading this don't. My kids are young, and life changes drastically as kids age, leave for college, then come back home after college while they try to get themselves established (just when you got used to being an empty-nester). Parents age and become new "children" to care for, bosses and jobs come and go, and circumstances change. So anything I might tell you in terms of details might not be much of a help.

The other alternative is to give you principles, theories, or rules-of-thumb that are general enough for you to adapt to your own circumstances. And yet, to simply relate a bunch of dry principles has never been my style. Theory is good, and I'm glad there are academics in the world who form new theories for us all to use, but I have a more practical bent. I like to know how things work—I like to be able to "see" how something is going to fit together. Probably too many puzzles in my early childhood and an anal-retentive gene somewhere in the mix (I'm sure there's a theory out there which explains it all). Either way, I like practical advice.

It was, therefore, somewhat of a dilemma for me to figure out how to say something useful about work-life balance when I was first approached to relate my views on the subject. I could talk about my current tricks, but they would only help those who shared my circumstances. I could talk about general theory, and leave everyone feeling like they'd been given a load of abstract gobblety-gook with nothing "real" behind it. It just wasn't clear what to do.

My solution: do both.

Five chapters of this book each describe a general principle, something I have learned either from the wonderful mentors who have helped me or else from my own life experiences, distilled down to a compact form. Why the theory? Because it's the only thing of lasting value I can pass along. I don't see how this kind of book would be useful without principles that anyone could apply at every stage of life, regardless of the circumstances. I get them said up front, right at the top of each chapter, and put them in an easy-to-find font. At the very end of the book, I provide a "Quick Reference" where you can see all the principles together, in bullet form, so you don't have to play "hunt and peck" when you want to come back to the book for a quick refresher.

Every chapter starts with a principle. Like most good theories, the principle is expressed in a succinct form which is great—once you already understand it. But just exactly why a principle exists may not be obvious. In fact, the principles I have written here may not even make sense the first time you read them. I sincerely hope not; many of them did not make sense to me at first, and it has only been my effort to embrace them that has fueled my ability to strike a balance in my life. If everything I have to say is already that blatantly obvious, then I'm not really doing anything for you. I guess that implies you can find out right now whether or not to buy this book—just thumb through the pages and read the principle at the top of each chapter. If your reaction is "ho hum," then do yourself a favor and put this down right now. Go spend the money on your kids.

After the principle-in-italics section at the top, I put on my "teacher hat" and try to express the reasoning behind the principle as best I can. That's what I am doing right now. At the top of this chapter I have a short paragraph, in italics, that describes the outline I have used for the chapters of this book. I'm now in my ninth paragraph explaining to you why I've chosen this approach (that is, if you count the one-sentence paragraph. My high school English teacher would never have let me get away with that, but she's not here to correct me, so I'm gonna count how I want to, use bad grammar, start sentences with "so" and, dare I say it, even use non-words like "gonna"). In the end, of course, I want to have done my level best to explain the principle to you in a way you can understand in your gut, so you can carry it around with you without having to memorize it. If I sprinkle in some of my own warped humor as I go, that's just my way of making this fun for me and of putting in just enough quirkiness that you might crack a smile as you go. Work-life balance can be a grim subject; I see a lot of tired looking folks out there, and it only seems to be getting harder. You might even have bought this book because you feel you're at the end of your rope. God knows I can relate to that feeling. But if I get too serious too often, it will all sound too depressing or, worse, it will come across as preachy. And if that happens, then I will get depressed about this project and never finish it. Besides, a smile never hurt anybody.

OK, that's enough said about the "principle" part of each chapter. You get it. But that's only the first half of each chapter. As I said before, principle is great, but in the end I want to say something practical too. That's why after explaining each principle, I follow up with one or more stories that I hope will bring the principle to life. My secret hope is that you will begin thinking of your own stories as you go. Perhaps you will even form a group of like-minded friends who are struggling along with the same issues you are and swap stories. Story telling is as old as humanity and one of the greatest gifts we have to give each other. I find that when I am struggling, nothing helps quite as much as hearing someone else's story. It is often just the inspiration I need to keep going. Here, then, is a simple story to go along with this chapter.

Story: It's Work-Life Balanc*ing*

There's no such thing as work-life balance. It should be work-life balanc*ing*, because it's never finished. There is no magic "balanced state" from which everything else is a deviation. That would be like thinking of marriage as a wedding. What a bizarre thought! Marriage isn't a one-time event that happens on some special day; it's an every day event. One doesn't "get married;" one is either married or not. It's something that requires continual, active participation. Work-life balancing is the same way. It's more of a constant juggling act, an on-going adjustment, where, from time to time, you admit to yourself "you know, I'm tired of such-and-such kicking my butt—it's time to revisit that topic and try something new."

A great example for us (my wife and I) is the "morning routine." This is that time between the regaining of consciousness and the unpacking of your briefcase at your desk. You know what I'm talking about: showering, bathroom ballet around who's going to use the sink first, picking out the clothes, walking the dog, emptying the trash, making the lunches for school, feeding the cats, retrieving the paper from where it landed in the puddle under the thorn bush—and having it all work out so that when you do finally get to work your socks actually match and you don't collapse from exhaustion. I don't know how it is for everyone else, but I can't think of any other aspect of our lives that has changed so often.

Before children, before pets, before we became home owners, it seemed like such a simple thing. About 45 minutes to get yourself ready and then out the door you go. If I was ambitious, I would wake up a bit earlier and get in a workout before heading to the office, maybe pick up one of those vitamin shakes on the way in. Either way, the morning routine was easy and I never really gave it much thought or preparation.

Of course, children changed all that.

First, it turned into our own version of "Survivor." After being up four times during the night for a feeding, the morning routine was more of a test of sheer will power than anything else. We went through several phases of trying to figure out the best way to clean the bottles, which had their own elaborate microwave sterilization routine that left them far too hot to handle (on the plus side, this was *very* effective at waking you up at 3 in the morning and I'm sure my daughters learned some choice vocabulary words that will help them fit right in when they miss that 2 foot put on 17). I have a dim memory of an attempt to use a wooden bottle rack for drying the bottles which ended in a disaster when I realized, one bleary-eyed morning, that the water from the bottles was seeping into cracks in the wood and feeding an ever growing colony of mold.

"Honey...what do you think is giving the baby digestive problems?"
"Gee, I dunno...could be the MOLD FROM THE BOTTLE RACK!"

I ask you…a wooden bottle rack…who thought *that* was a good idea?

As the kids got older, and we enrolled them in day care, there was a whole lot more prep work to the morning routine. Now it wasn't just about getting ourselves cleaned up, dressed, and fed, but also about doing that for two other people.[1] Added to that were all the new tasks that popped up each morning, such as when somebody yanked off a sock which you then had to find, or when that bowl of cereal got knocked to the floor which you then had to clean up, or the having to chase someone around the house who thought the "running around naked game" was more fun than humans should be allowed to have. And of course, the commute to work got longer because someone had to drop the kids off and pick them up from day care which, in turn, meant a compressed work schedule. So in order to get more out of each hour at work, you decided that you would bring a sack lunch and eat at your desk. But that, of course, meant that you had to pack a lunch, which added yet another task to your morning routine and left even less time for the running around naked game.

About the time we finally got *that* routine figured out, everything changed. My oldest entered kindergarten which meant that we now had a completely different time when we had to get her to school. Moreover, now there were two drop off and pick up locations (instead of just one) that had to be incorporated into the commute routine. And then there were the rules—the never ending parade of rules—

---

[1] At least when they are babies you can just slap a diaper on them and let them crawl around on the floor. Sure they get dirty, but dads don't care about that so much. After all, that's what baths are for.

that go with grade school. Sometimes I think the only purpose of grade schools is to invent rules and print them out on colored paper in an obscure font and send them home to torture working parents. Or perhaps it's not the grade school at all but the bored state legislators that have nothing better to do than add even more bureaucracy to our overly-regulated education system. Either way, there's nothing quite like coming home from a long day's work to a pile of multi-colored paper from the grade school informing you that morning assembly starts at precisely 7:36 am, or that parking is no longer allowed on the street behind the school between the hours of 6:49 and 8:07 on weekdays, unless it is a school holiday (see the pink sheet from last week for details on the school calendar—you kept it, of course).

But I digress. The point is simply this: things change and you have to be open to changing with them. If you get upset when something upsets your apple cart, you are in for a long haul. But if, instead, you take the view that there is no single answer, no one formula that represents "having it all," you will be doing yourself a huge favor. When you see that parent who looks so fit, so together, with the perfectly groomed children, you will find you won't have to fight down a wild urge to run over and smack that smirk off their smug little face. You'll find instead you walk with a lighter step, happy with yourself because *you* are proud of the progress *you* are making in *your* own life and looking forward to that upcoming evening *you* have planned for being alone with *your* spouse. And you may even find, like I have, that when you aren't spending so much time beating yourself up for not being perfect, you get much better at noticing the tricks other people are using for balancing their own lives. That's one of the great things about work-life balancing: plagiarism isn't an issue. If you see someone who looks "together" go strike up a conversation and steal any good ideas they will give you.

So read on. I've organized the chapters to focus on the five principles that I use all the time. They make a huge difference for me; I hope you find them as useful in your life.

Why Should You Care What I Say?

You need a reason to believe what I am saying. You need hard evidence showing what I say really works.

It occurred to me that you might not give a darn about what I have to say. After all, why would you? I'm not a trained psychologist. I'm not a university researcher who has spent years studying this problem with reams of carefully collected data to back me up. I'm just a regular guy, pursuing the same goals as millions of other people: a rewarding career and a loving family. I am, in short, "nothing special." And so it begs the question: why should anyone listen to anything I have to say on the topic of work-life balancing? Why should you care what I say? The answer: precisely because I *am* so unremarkable. I'm just like you, and yet I've been able to achieve a lifestyle that many of my friends and acquaintances have told me is, in fact, remarkable.

The point is, if I can do it, you can. And perhaps it's refreshing to hear from a "regular person" about how to make work-life work well. I don't have any special training or degrees that make me different. There is no scar on my forehead that has left me with magical powers. My wife and I don't have access to any special resources or circumstances. No hidden fortune in our family's past allows me to sit at home and eat bon-bons. And although I am white and male, I can assure you there is no such thing as an "old boy network" that has made life a slam dunk for me. If someone thinks there is, I wish they would please send me a letter and let me know how to get in, because apparently I missed the memo.

Just like you, I face the same morning routines, the same sick kids that take me away from work, the same worries over aging parents, the same pressures to produce at work, the same angst over whether I am spending enough time with my kids, the same wish to have more time to spend with my friends or in my community, and the same occasional wild desires to "chuck it all" and just take off running with a credit card until they catch me and put me away.

But as with anything else, the proof is in the pudding. For my opinion to have any meaning, any weight, it has to be backed up with evidence. It's no different from anything else. We all tend to "believe it when we see it." If I'm an ordinary guy who has been able to achieve an extraordinary lifestyle, you need to hear some proof. You need a feel for what I have been able to do with my life to get a feel for why the ideas in this book would have any real meaning for you.

The best proof I could think of giving you is to tell you about my own life over the last year. It amounts to putting myself in a position close to bragging, which I am not comfortable doing. But maybe I can do it without sounding like a total horse's you-know-what. I'm going to try, at any rate, because it is the best example I can give you to prove that the ideas I have written down here are not just "nice things to try when you get the time" but really, truly, the principles that I live by every day. They do make a difference in what I am able to get done in my life. Perhaps if you see what I've been able to do, in the circumstances I live with, it will inspire you to read the rest of the book and give you a reason to believe these same principles can work for you too.

Story: A Year In My Life

Let's begin with the basic stats. I am an engineer-turned-manager. I work for IBM. My wife is a full-time attorney and also works in a full-time capacity (specifically, neither of us is part-time and neither of us job-share). We have two children, one in day care and the other in first grade. We have two cats, and live in a typical suburban style home.

All of this means we face many of the same pressures that millions of others face. The grass needs to be cut. The bushes need to be trimmed. The leaves have to be raked. The cats have to be taken to the vet. Somebody has to do the grocery shopping. Somebody has to pay the bills on time. We have to make lunches, pick out clothes, get breakfast ready, and convince tired children that they need to hurry if we are going to make it to school on time. Kids grow so quickly we have to go shopping for stuff it seems we bought just last week. We have bosses that have deadlines and who sometimes ask us to stay late. We have to clean the house, do the laundry, pick up the mess, monitor how much TV is being watched, and clean the cat box. We worry about money, how our wonderful politicians have made it 4 times more expensive to put a kid through college by sucking money away from education and sinking it into deficits, how Social Security will, in all likelihood, be gone by the time we grow old, and how to find time to play part-time investor for whatever we've been able to put away for retirement so we don't get totally screwed by the big boys at the professional investment houses. When something breaks, we have to make the weekend trip to the "do it yourself" store, which always turns into 10 *more* trips and a nightmare of working your way out of a maze of bad advice when the stupid little thing doesn't fit like they told you it would. And when all that doesn't work, just like you, we have to swallow our do-it-yourself pride and call in the professionals, waiting at home for them to show up "some time between 7 am and 4 pm," and then make up the time on the weekend answering the 50 emails that came in while we were making sure the guy who showed up to fix the problem did the job right so we don't end up having to call him out a second time.

Of course in our spare time, with our spare money, we get to do things for ourselves.

Sound familiar? Yeah, it's rough out there. What makes it worse is that nobody seems to care that much. On the contrary, we're given the clear message that no matter how hard we try we've not done enough. Our culture shouts at us that we are inadequate, and we'd better hurry up and part with even more of our money or we'll be a total loser. It only takes one walk through a grocery store check-out line to get a first-hand look at the never ending pounding we all take. Grocery store check-out lines have to be one of the nine planes of Hell. You're stuck, in a confined space, waiting your turn in a line that crawls. Everywhere you look are those magazines with the perfect, air-brushed pictures, haranguing you poor women about everything from the color of your hair, to the size of your waist (or other things), to the latest secrets for turning on your man so he won't just up and leave you one day. Honestly, I don't know how women take it; I'm not even a woman and there are days I just want to walk in with a flame thrower and reduce the magazine rack at the checkout line to a bubbling pile of goo. Perhaps that explains why I so often see women reading a book while they wait in line to pay for their groceries.

The point is, it can be depressing and you can find yourself feeling like giving up. Our culture today definitely does not create an environment that encourages balance. Yet, would you believe it's possible to avoid all this crap getting to you? Would you believe it's possible to feel like you have a million things to do, and still feel like you can get things done that *you* really want to do? Can you imagine a day when you would *welcome* the fact that your life is filled to overflowing because you feel like it gives you *more* opportunities to do what you like? That's what life is like for me, and it can be that way for you.

Come to think of it now, perhaps I did have an unfair advantage. I grew up with a father who was a heart surgeon and worked 24x7. He was an awesome dad and I wouldn't trade him for the world, but he was a work-a-holic. That had two profound effects on me. First, I am a "type-A" personality. No use denying it. I definitely want to achieve great things if I can. I saw my Dad do great things, watched him literally save peoples' lives, and saw the fulfillment he got from it. I believe most of us want to make a difference. Money is great, but mattering is more important. As I watched my Dad, I decided early on that I wanted to be like him and leave the world a better place than I had found it. I don't see the point of working if I'm not making a difference.

17

The other impact of my father's life on me was that I got to see the effects first hand of an "always on" world, long before such a world became the latest fashion. Everything today is "on line." Our technical marvels have made it possible for us to answer email in bed, or to be on vacation on a remote island and still participate in conference calls. "Always on" can also be "never off." A generation ago, my Dad was already living that life. He felt he had little time for anything else beyond his work, and it wasn't pretty for him. He loved his family deeply, yet he missed out on a lot because of the choices he felt compelled to make. I had a front row seat to that show, and got to hear him relate to me, late in his life, how much he regretted it.

As a consequence, I made the decision long ago that I would have a great career *and* I would have lots of interaction with my family. I never questioned the desire to have both things, never questioned that having both simultaneously is possible. It's just an assumption that has become part my internal reality. When that internal view doesn't match with the real world, I assume something is wrong with the real world and push at it until it changes to fit my needs. And it always does. I sometimes have to be creative and do things differently, but that has become part of the fun.

With that as a backdrop, what follows are the highlights of my last 12 months. I work in a group at IBM called "Extreme Blue." We run innovation projects on open questions that confront the company in new or emerging markets, and select small teams to focus on finding answers to those questions. My job is to select the projects and get them set up so they have the greatest chance of succeeding. We run three cycles a year and the projects are paid for by sponsors who expect great results. We drive ourselves to achieve those results by putting on high profile "show case events" at the end of each cycle. As with any innovation program, we have the challenge of showing meaningful return on investment, which can be tough when you are working on issues that have never been solved before. The result is that it always seems like we have a critical issue before us. In that situation it is easy to feel like one is always in a crisis.

Here's where it gets interesting. Despite my all-consuming "day job" I was able to get a bunch more done. I led one of several IBM working groups participating on a nation-wide study looking at innovation implications for the U.S. in the next century. I led another working group participating on an internal IBM study looking at intellectual property issues as they relate to innovation. I participated in yet a third study, again internal to IBM, looking at our innovation culture across the company. I participated as a panel member on a fourth IBM study, this one world-wide, examining the global outlook for innovation. In all, I made five trips to Europe, one trip to China, and probably a half-dozen trips within the U.S. During this same year, I also wrote a book—not this one, this is my second foray into authorship (my other book is on the topic of—surprise!—innovation). And finally, last but not least, I also managed to take three vacations during this same time period.

"OK, great" you might say. "So you got a lot done at work. But you must have paid a price. Surely you never saw your family and your wife did all the work around the house." Not so. During the last year my work schedule has been 8:30 to 6, and I almost never work on nights or weekends (I can literally count on one hand the number of times I spent doing work after hours or on a weekend). I make the lunches for my kids every morning. My wife makes them breakfast while I help them get dressed. I drive both of them to school every morning; my wife picks them up in the evening. I spend a couple of hours with my kids after work, most recently spending that time riding bikes with my older daughter whom I taught to ride a bike a few weeks ago. I am there for bath time and to read them stories every night (except when I travel, and I try to limit most of my trips to one night away). I do the grocery shopping every week; my wife pays the bills. I typically get in three or four workouts a week.

Does my wife do more? Yes. When I travel she has to carry the whole load and there's no making up for that. But on a regular basis, we do our best to split it "half-sies" and I find that to be entirely manageable. In fact, it's more than manageable; I would call it essential. How else is my wife supposed to have the life and career she wants? And if she can't do that, how is she supposed to be happy? And if she's unhappy, how would that impact me? So, yeah, I do the grocery shopping though I suppose there are some Neanderthals out there who think I'm less of a man for doing so. My wife and I also manage to find time to go out on weekly "date nights." And to top it off, I managed to find a way to give her a week by herself in the summer without the kids or me which I hope at least partially made up for all the extra work she had to do when I was traveling.

The point is not to brag and I hope I haven't come across as a bore. Rather, my goal is to show you that this kind of life is possible. More importantly, since I am "nothing special," then if I can do it, anyone can. In fact, I think it should be the way we all live our lives. One would tend to think that "something would have to give," either the career would have to take a back seat or the family would. That's the standard thinking. It's what we've all been taught. And it's not true. I'm not saying I don't have to make choices; that would be a lie. But the point is that I can make *different choices* than you might imagine (like doing the grocery shopping) and still have the things I want in my life. I don't have to swallow the party line and buckle to what my culture says is "the right thing to do." I can, and do, ignore that cultural noise that is splashed across the magazine rack and go my own way.

In what follows, I will share with you the principles I use to keep my life in balance. There are five of them in all. Some are things you may have heard before; others will take a bit more explaining. Each comes with one or more true stories of how I've applied them in my life. Taken together, they represent the blueprint I use to make the engine of my life run the way I want it to run.

"So what," you might counter, "maybe you're just a freak of nature and these principles only work for you." I don't think so, and neither do the many people I've coached on work-life balance using the ideas outlined in this book.

1   **Be Process Oriented**

Principle 1: Make a fundamental paradigm shift to being process oriented versus outcome obsessed. Most of us interpret a desire to be "goal oriented" to mean the end result is everything. That is a mistake. Results are critical, but you must focus on the process, not the end-game, and let the results come to you.

It's an All-The-Time Thing

I heard it said once that Vince Lombardi, the famous football coach of the Green Bay Packers, has been terribly misquoted in his famous saying "winning isn't everything, it's the only thing." The correct quote, supposedly, was "winning is not a sometimes thing, it's an all-the-time thing."

Whether or not the story of the misquote is true, I love the latter quote: "winning is an all-the-time thing." Perhaps it's not as snappy, certainly it's not as controversial as the usual quote, but it sure hits a bull's eye when it comes to one of the things I find particularly wrong with American culture today. We are way too focused on results. And the irony of it all is this: if you really want to get to a result, the key is *not* to dwell on it.

If this sounds counter intuitive, well, I admit it. It is counter intuitive. After all, we all know that what matters are results, right? We live in a market-based society and work in jobs where "the bottom line" is what is important. Most of us face evaluations of some sort that govern our pay increases, our bonuses, and whether or not we get promoted. Moreover, we all reinforce this kind of results-oriented thinking every time we comparison shop and select a product or service because it has a superior brand or because the price is lower than the competition's. So results do, in fact, matter. I am not about to come across as some granola-happy slacker who thinks we should all go back to nature, live in a commune, and everything will magically take care of itself. That might be a nice vision, but I recognize it is not reality. Results are what we are judged by and there's no getting around it.

Truth be told, I would not want to get around being judged by results. Like most guys, I like competition. Achieving a result is a blast and I love the sense of accomplishment I feel when I hit a goal I've been working towards. Just this past Thanksgiving, I finally succeeded in teaching my older daughter how to ride a bicycle. It was one of those rare "Norman Rockwell" kinds of moments, with the grandparents watching and the video camera rolling. The feeling was unbelievable and the look on her face—the light in her eyes—said it all. Avoiding results would mean losing out on moments like that. Who would want such a life?

But where we make our mistake (myself included, by the way) is when the result comes to dominate our thinking as the only important thing. Even that isn't stated correctly; the result *is* important—the mistake comes from thinking so much about the result that *the result becomes*

24

what you do. Stop and think about that a moment and you will see it makes absolutely no sense at all. A result is a *point in time*, the *end* of a series of *actions.* It has absolutely no impact in terms of getting you anywhere. Focusing on worrying about hitting a home run, for example, does nothing to help you actually hit the home run. Simply put, a result is not an action and, therefore, cannot help you make progress.

For example, imagine I am baking a cake for my wife's birthday, and I'm really worried about making it come out perfectly. If I sit in my kitchen and say to myself over and over "I've got to bake a perfect cake! I've got to bake a perfect cake!" then nothing will actually get done. I'll just be sitting in my kitchen, holding my head in my hands, worrying about the outcome.[2] No baking will actually get done. Thinking about a result, and *dwelling* on it, does nothing for actually moving you forward towards achieving a result. In fact, it *holds you back* by wasting your valuable time and energy. Being results-oriented is, ironically, counter productive to actually achieving a result!

By contrast, a process-centric view (or action-centric, if you prefer that language) concentrates your energies around things you can actually do—actions *you* can take that will move *you* in the direction *you* want to go. Even if you want to hit a particular result, some particular goal by some deadline, the only way to get there is by *taking actions*! A process-centric view concentrates your thought

---

[2] I realize my example is simplistic, but are you honest enough to admit to ever wasting time obsessing ridiculously about an outcome? You know, like losing sleep the night before a big event, or worrying about whether someone will care about that tie you picked out? Yep...me too. Been there, done that.

and effort on taking the actions that you believe will maximize your chances of reaching your goal. More importantly, and this is where you get the work-life balancing boost, if you are process-centered you *avoid wasting time and energy* worrying about outcomes—time and energy you can then sink back into taking the actions that will increase your chances of hitting your goal.

Now, think back to the story I told in the last chapter about how I am able to get so much more done that other people in the same period of time. Do you see now one of the main reasons why I can do that? It's because I'm not wasting my time and energy worrying. I am literally more productive because I'm not wasting the gobs of time that, in a former life, used to weigh me down like a ball-and-chain. I'm not any more capable than anyone else; I've just learned a secret to being more efficient. It's as though we are all running a marathon, and everyone else is carrying a 70-lb pack that I learned how to drop a long time ago.

Athletics can give us great analogies for being process oriented versus outcome obsessed. Say my goal is to beat a personal best for a one-mile run. In fact, say I have to beat that personal best within a given period of time (like one track season) because it is the only way I can qualify to advance to my state finals. So this is a very specific goal, with dire results if I don't hit my target. Given such circumstances, it would be natural to judge myself on how close I am to beating that mark. That makes sense, right? Every day I shave off a second or two from my time is a day of accomplishment. Every day I get a bit slower is a reminder to redouble my efforts. It all makes sense; it's what anyone would do. But it is flat wrong! Why? Because on any given day my mile time might vary by as much as 15 seconds, depending upon a host of inputs over which I have no control: the wind, how strong I felt, how slippery the track was, etc. If I judge myself by the time on the clock, my self esteem will bounce around based on those conditions over which I have no control. That makes no sense at all. Instead, I should judge myself by the *actions* I am taking. Am I warming up properly? Am I eating properly? Am I getting to bed on time? Is my workout routine at the proper pace so I will know how it feels when I am running at the right pace? These are all things I can control, and they are all actions I can take. If I warm up properly, after a good night's rest, and can maintain a relaxed form at the pace I know (from my workouts) feels at or faster than the desired pace, then my goal will follow. It is inevitable. Moreover, it's the *only way* my goal can be achieved and anything else amounts to a negative impact. When athletes talk about being "in the zone" this is what they mean; they have reached a relaxed state of mind where *the actions they know they need to take are happening without resistance*. Their mind is completely freed of outcome so it can be totally focused on process.

"OK," you say, "but what if my information isn't perfect? What if I'm not sure what actions I should take? Shouldn't I spend the time to figure out what the right actions should be?" Yes...and no. Yes, you should, of course, try to do some research to get a feel for what actions will most efficiently move you where you want to go. And certainly you should keep tabs on your progress to give you feedback on whether your chosen actions seem to be working or whether you might experiment with different actions. But no, you should not obsess about making sure you understand absolutely every possible angle before you get started. That would be the same thing as obsessing on results; you'd be obsessing on "the perfect plan" and you would never get started on anything. Remember that even if you get it wrong and your actions take you the wrong way, *that is progress in itself.* You will have eliminated a possibility which clears the way for you to take the right action. If you stay honest with yourself and evaluate your progress towards your desired result, you will be able to catch a "wrong" action early on, make a correction, and quickly eliminate those activities that take you the wrong way. You can "fail fast" which will only speed you on your way to the ultimate place you want to be.

Beware of Expectations

I want to be clear about something here. In this chapter, I have not talked at all about how to choose your goals. I will have a lot more to say on that topic in subsequent chapters, especially Chapter 3. What I have done is to emphasize that the best path towards *any* goal you select is through avoiding results and concentrating on process. I do, however, want to take one tiny peek ahead and offer a word of warning about *expectations*, especially those expectations you place upon yourself. Expectations are trouble. They should be considered your mortal enemy. Tattoo that on the inside of your forehead and never forget it.

Expectations are, by their vary nature, arbitrary. They are statements about the future, as in "if I hire you for this job I *expect* you to increase profits" or "here is your sales quota and I *expect* you to hit it." As statements about the future, expectations are unpredictable because, of course, nobody knows what the future will bring. The point is to make sure you don't get sucked in to judging yourself by expectations. *Don't buy-in to other people's expectations!* That is the same as being outcome obsessed. When you hear yourself saying things like "I should have done this by now" or "I'm 40 years old and I should have earned my first million by now" you will know that you are buying in to other people's expectations. At that point you have fallen off the wagon and are back in to being outcome obsessed. Blow off the expectations, and reset your thinking on the process you want to pursue to maximize your chances of reaching the goals you care about the most.[3]

Point of view is everything here; you have to relish the actions themselves and avoid beating yourself up because your timeline for progress isn't exactly what you imagined it would be. Progress towards a result should be used like a probe to tell you which actions to take. It should never be used as a judgment of your self worth. The idea is to teach yourself how to feel good about what you *are doing*, not what you have done or might achieve. In a sense, it becomes a statement of faith versus an attitude of control. You focus on tuning your actions, making yourself as good a *performer* as you can be, and you put your faith in the notion that good results will follow good performance. So it's not "I've got to bake the perfect cake" but rather "I'm going to focus on being the best baker I can be and I'm sure the best cake I can possibly make will come out of that process."

Here's the moral of the story. If you dwell on results, then winning becomes a sometimes thing. You will only feel good about yourself on those few occasions when you are receiving an award or holding a trophy. The *only way* for winning to be an all-the-time thing is if you are process oriented. To be sure, let the results guide which actions

---

[3] For practical advice on how to avoid expectations, see the "Rule of Judgment" on pg 134.

you pick to be part of your process, but learn how to get your jollies from what you do, not from what you achieve. You will find you are not only happier, but that you also get way more accomplished.

Story: Little Drops of Water, Little Grains of Sand

Little drops of water
Little grains of sand
Make the mighty oceans
And the pleasant land

My father related the above to me as one of the favorite sayings he learned from his father. It has become one of my own favorites. I never met my grandfather, but he was just like millions of other hard-working immigrants who made (and continue to make) our country great. He came here from Greece, learned English, served in the military, set up his own shop, saved his money and put his children through school so they could have a better life. I love this saying from him, not only because it's a link to a cherished and admired ancestor, but also because it so neatly captures the essence of *process*. It teaches that what matters in life comes from the little things you do moment-to-moment, day-in and day-out. Big results come from small activities. All the action is in the process.

The best way I can illustrate the benefits of this kind of thinking is to talk about what I am doing right now: writing a book. This is actually my second foray into the arena of authorship, and when my long time mentor George Dempsey first introduced me to the idea I thought he was insane. "Write a book?" I said "what are you, kidding me?"

30

A book, after all, is a huge undertaking, right? It takes hours of time. I had images in my mind of someone holed up in a cabin in the woods, hammering away on a type writer, hoping not to go insane from writer's block. OK, maybe I was overly influenced from watching *The Shining* but still, a book seemed like something that took dedicated time—something that you had to devote yourself to doing for long, uninterrupted periods.

And for me, that was an impossibility. I am the father of two small children, one still in preschool. And as any parent knows, that stage in life takes a lot of attention. It's a 24x7 kind of existence; when you aren't working at your job you are helping your kids or trying to make up for feeling guilty that you haven't spent more time with them. This is not to say it's not enjoyable—it is—but the one thing you don't have is long stretches of uninterrupted time. I can recall, about 10 B.C.,[4] being bored (a dim, distant memory) and feeling like I had nothing better to do than waste some time watching an old movie on TV. Children changed all that. Writing a book seemed like something completely incompatible with the lifestyle of a working dad (or mom). Yet here I am, writing a book, and there you are reading the results of that effort, all of which accomplished during what will probably be the busiest and most hectic time of my life. To me, there is no better example of the power of process.

So how does that work, exactly? How do I "fit it in" among everything else? The key is process (surprise) and thinking in the here-and-now as opposed to the future. As I write this sentence, I am spending the first hour of my day writing. I get up an hour before the morning mayhem starts

---

[4] B.C. stands for "before children"

and literally set a timer. I plug in a set of head phones with some music stored on my computer that I find makes for great background. And I write. I simply focus on whatever part of the book I happen to be the most charged up about at the moment. Right now, it's relating this story to you as an example of the power of process. I have the grammar checker turned off, the spell checker turned off, and the magnification set at about 150% (I wear contacts but it is way, way too early for me to put them in yet). What comes out is large and misspelled, but I don't care about that. I know there will be a time in the future for spell checking and rewriting. All I am interested in right now is getting words on the page. I have all the information in my head and the biggest challenge, right now, is to get something started.

Most importantly, as I write these words I have absolutely no idea how or even whether this book will get done, nor whether anyone will ever read it or find it helpful. I also have no idea yet about how many chapters I will have, nor even if this story will remain in this chapter or be moved somewhere else. That's not important because it's not something I need to control. So I put it out of my mind. But I don't ignore the fact that I certainly *want* people to buy the book and find it helpful. I simply recognize the futility of focusing on something that will only waste my time. Instead, I think about what I can control, the actual act of writing, and that *as long as I am writing I am making the best progress I can make.*

So I'm not talking some namby-pamby, feel-good-about-the-process-and-never-think-at-all-about-the-results attitude here. I definitely do want to finish the book, definitely do want to have it sell. The goals are part of the reality and you can't take them out of the equation. The difference is that dwelling on the outcome is pointless. It doesn't get me there any faster. Worse, it wastes my energy and can sap my enthusiasm. If I spend my time worrying about the near impossible task of getting this published, it could be enough to drown me. Instead, I admit the two things that are simple truths: I have a goal I want to reach, and there are many steps to take to reach that goal. Every word has to be written, spell checked, read and reread, etc. I can know that I am doing my level best to reach a goal, even when the goal is uncertain. So even if I have no control over the outcome, I have total control over the actions I can take to maximize my potential of reaching that desired outcome. That means I can be "winning all the time"—literally every moment I spend writing is a victory.

The wonderful thing is how this sort of attitude feeds on itself. Once you get into this groove, it gets easier and easier to continue "winning," which amounts to living your life in a way that you feel empowered. As I write this, I am doing something I like, something I believe in, something that I will feel proud of even if nobody else gives a tinker's damn. Why? Because I know I've done it with style and I've thrown myself into the best process I can devise. In short, if it is at all possible that I can write a book on work-life balancing and get it published, this is exactly the right way to go about doing it. I have already won, because I am doing everything I can to maximize my chance of success.

Story: Making Progress By Going the Wrong Way

One of the things that used to bug me was wondering whether I was taking the right actions. When I was first introduced to process-oriented thinking, I could at least understand how taking actions was the gateway to results, but what about taking an action that ends up being the wrong thing? Don't you have to worry about that? After all, isn't doing the wrong thing, which would take you in the opposite direction of where you should be going, worse than not taking any action at all? How can you have any faith at all in the notion that taking an action, even a wrong one, is still going to lead to progress? If you follow the logic out, then you end up trying to predict every possible outcome in advance, foresee every move and counter move, so you can know which action you should be taking. And then you are right back to being results-obsessed, spending all your time thinking about possible outcomes before you can even begin to act. So isn't being process oriented just the same as being results obsessed?

No. Hard as it may be to believe, taking almost any action can help. My brush with medical school is a perfect example.

My Dad was a heart surgeon, and like many kids, I wanted to emulate my father, so for a long time I thought I wanted to be a doctor. The feeling lingered with me throughout college. When I selected my major (Computer Science) I made sure to leave room in my schedule to take all the pre-med classes as well. I took biology, chemistry, and organic chemistry, even though none of these topics counted towards my major, because doing so left the door open for me to apply to medical school.

Six years after college and well into a career with NASA, I still wondered about being a doctor. I eventually decided to take an MCAT prep class (the MCAT is the medical school entrance exam). I even spent the time and money to fly myself back to talk with my former professors to secure good letters of recommendation for my medical school applications. Interestingly, one of my former professors wisely suggested that I spend some time volunteering at a local hospital, in various departments, just as a way to get a feel for the kinds of work I might want to do.

I came back to Houston, began filling out my medical school applications, and volunteered in a local heart patient intensive care ward. After about a month, I came to a realization that brought the whole thing to a halt: I don't like sick people; or rather, I don't like being around sick people. Kind of a bad thing if you want to be a doctor, wouldn't you say? I found that my favorite time at the hospital was about when the patient was getting ready to leave. Up to that point, I really didn't want to be around somebody who wasn't feeling very well and wasn't in the mood to chat. I like interacting with people, particularly with humor, and the hospital is not the ideal setting for joking around with patients ("Hey how you feeling today? Gee…that feeding tube looks like it hurts." Not good.)

So the whole thing was a waste of time, right? Worse, I spent a fair sum paying for the MCAT prep course, and flying myself back to college, not to mention the hours I put in relearning chemistry and biology so I could take the 8-hour MCAT exam. And pay for that as well. Not only did I not end up being a doctor, I could have avoided the investment of time and money to figure that out if I had thought to volunteer at the hospital as a first step. A colossal waste of time and money, right?

Not at all. I have no regrets, and the process gave me an indispensable gift: it freed me from something that had been on my mind for a long time. It was liberating to finally realize I really didn't want to be a doctor after all, something that had been nagging at me for a good 15 years.

35

Now, sure, I could have been smarter about figuring things out. I could have volunteered at the hospital first. Yet the thought never occurred to me until I spoke with a former professor who suggested it, and I never would have spoken with that professor if I hadn't gotten serious about getting my medical school application together. If I hadn't already invested the money in an MCAT prep course, would I have had the resolve to fly myself back to my college campus to talk to that professor? Certainly not. So I admit the route I took was not optimal, but the point is that I made progress. I never look back any more; I never wonder if I would have been happier as a doctor. I know the answer to that question is "no." More importantly, *I had to get that answer before I could get on with my life.* If you had told me back then that I would be writing books on work-life balancing, I would have looked at you cross-eyed. And yet, if I had not eliminated the doctor option, it could easily have remained a distraction that might have prevented me from ever writing this book. You just never know.

Think of it this way: ask yourself how much time you have spent wondering about doing something without actually taking any action. For example, how many hours would you say you have spent thinking about how much better you would feel if you had a regular workout routine? How many times have you wondered how much more rewarding your marriage might be if you and your spouse made it a priority to spend at least one night a week together going out for dinner without the kids? How many nights have you spent on a lonely business trip, eating dinner by yourself, thinking that there must be some way for you to spend more time with your kids? Now take all those hours back and imagine yourself *actually trying something.* Try anything; it doesn't even matter what you try first. Would it really be a loss if what you tried didn't work out? How could it possibly be a "failure" if, by taking an action, you at least eliminated a possibility and moved on to the next idea? Could it be any more of a waste than all those hours you've already thrown away all those hours without doing a darn thing? By taking an action, you will inevitably hit on some formula that works for you. To me, trying something is a helluva lot better than sitting around wondering. And if you aren't so concerned with outcome, but instead are giving yourself pats on the back for being engaged in a process you know will eventually bring results, you don't have to care about failure! In fact, failure takes on a whole new meaning; instead of being negative, it becomes positive, as in "ok, that didn't work. Now I get to try something else."

Story: Nobody Ever Hit a Milestone By Focusing On It

Project management is serious business at IBM. Project managers are those folks who are charged with ensuring that a given project comes in "on time and under budget" or as close to that Holy Grail as is possible. Becoming certified as a project manager is a coveted prize at IBM, and an IBM project management certification is highly regarded in the industry in general. Many employees put in long hours of training to achieve the certification and subsequently make a career out of the proper handling of projects. All of which is why I was so surprised, when I took my first IBM project management class, to hear my instructor say that "it is impossible to manage to a milestone."

We were about half way through the introductory course on project management. As part of that course, we learn a variety of techniques that are useful for tracking the progress of a project. The procedure is quite elaborate and extremely powerful. By taking certain systematic actions, one can literally "plot out" the course of a project, map dependencies among the various groups and activities that will be involved with achieving success, and even find those elements of the plan that are going to be bottlenecks. All of this gives the project manager insight as to where to focus his or her efforts to ensure the overall project stays on track.

After going through an extremely detailed analysis of an example project case study, our class had identified a particularly nasty bottleneck. It was, I am sure, meant to come out that way, and to get us thinking about what we would do if faced with a project where one or more key events had to happen on time for the whole thing to be a success. Having identified the problem and, as a class, agreed upon the pivotal milestone, our instructor asked us to discuss the issue. How could we ensure the project's success? What could we do to make sure we hit that key milestone? She asked us flat out, "given the critical nature of this milestone, that you have all identified, how many of you think your most important job will be to manage this milestone?"

Naturally we all raised our hands, which was when she said, "No, that is not your most important job! *You can't manage a milestone; you can only manage the processes that lead up to it.*"

Think about that and you will see it is profound. The whole class was focused on the importance of the milestone, as we have all come to learn in our culture. Hitting the milestone was important—we had literally just proved that fact—and so it drew all of our attention. We were laser focused on making sure that happened. And, because we are all so well-trained to be results-obsessed, we completely blew it when the instructor asked us about the best way to hit the milestone. What she was pointing out was that we should not be *blinded* by the importance of the milestone. We should not forget that we could not really do anything about the *event*; our only control came from focusing on the *processes* before the event and making sure they were running smoothly. Yes the event was critical, but you would never get anywhere dwelling on it. Time spent worrying about a milestone was time wasted. Our only hope would be to focus on the processes that were up stream, since those were the only things we could control. We might still fail (who can predict the future?) but at least we would know we had done everything we could and had focused our energy in the right place.

There was one other important lesson I took away from this exercise. It turned out that many different processes led to the critical milestone. In some cases, there were alternatives to the processes that could be imagined as "backup plans." The result was liberating for me, because it showed me that I could focus my energies in any number of places and still make progress. If I had a good idea to improve one process, I could work on that even if some other process was giving me fits. By analogy to how I wrote this book, it is like saying that I could work on whatever story I felt the most inspired to write about on any given day. Eventually, all the stories had to get written for the book to be complete (the milestone) but the order in which I focused on writing them was not important. So I could leverage my strengths *at the moment*, rather than beating myself up if I wasn't inspired on some story or had hit a block. It allowed me to wake up, sit down at the computer, and get started right away on doing something useful. Certainly there were some parts of the book which I knew would be harder, where I wasn't sure I had good words to describe the principles, let alone enough good stories to illustrate it. And clearly I couldn't avoid them forever, but I could wait to take them on when I felt up to it. The point is this: you don't have to know everything to be making progress. If you focus on process, you will have many places you can make a difference.

From a work-life balancing perspective, this is great news. Look around at your overly complicated life. You'll see many things you will want to improve. Just pick one— it doesn't matter what you pick. Whatever you do on any given day will be a step towards a more balanced life.

2 | Live Blame-Free

Principle 2: Commit to living your life completely without "blame." Do this by taking the phrase "I can't" out of you vocabulary and substituting "I want" instead. This will give you a powerful tool for breaking out of the beliefs that are holding you back.

The One Thing I <u>Never</u> Needed to Know I Learned in Kindergarten

When it comes right down to it, the most powerful force working against your work-life balance is probably you. Happy thought, eh? And you were hoping there was a boogey man out there, somebody with a smoking gun that you could point to and say "there he is! It's *his* fault my life is a mess. GET HIM!" Instead, here I am telling you that everything you need to make your life what you want it to be is already something you possess if you would only get out of your own way. "Great," you say, "that's just jolly. So not only is my life not where I want it to be, but now Paul is telling me it's my own damn fault. Excuse me...why did I pay for this?"

Before you slam the book down in disgust, consider this: *you were duped.* You *do* have all the tools to make your life what you want it to be, but you were *never taught* how to use them to suit *your* purposes. Worse, what you *were* taught was to think in a way that specifically holds you back. And of course you aren't alone; all your classmates were taught the same things. The result is a whole culture surrounding you that reinforces some particularly nasty habits that are so commonplace we don't even recognize them as bad habits. They look "normal" which makes them both nasty and insidious. It means you will not only have to change the way you think, you will also have to go against the grain. People will laugh. They will say you are wrong. You will feel awkward. Even your closest family and friends will be skeptical. That's tough for anyone because we all like to fit in. And it's all because somewhere along the way we missed out on an important lesson, and we've spent the bulk of our lives reinforcing behavior that keeps us from discovering it.

The good news is there is a process for breaking out of this rut and I'm going to share it with you. But first, how do we learn these bad habits?

Please "Them"

The way I figure it, it all starts in kindergarten. There you are, separated for the first time from your family for extended periods, dropped off in a room full of strangers, with a person about four times your size who is in charge. A daunting situation for anyone, let alone someone at the ripe old age of five. You learn one lesson pretty quick and you learn it to your core: *please the teacher or die.* Anyone who has gone through dropping kids off at kindergarten (or day care) can attest to the tears. After all, you are 5 years old which is 13 years away from being able to live on your own terms (if you're lucky), and although everyone is pleasant and truly looking out for you, you are clearly dependent upon them. Quite literally, you must have others' help if you are to survive to adulthood. It's the world's original game of "survivor" and some of the competitors bite when they get upset.

Lesson number one, then, is to *please them*; specifically, the teacher. She[5] tells you what to do, when you can eat, when you can play, when you can nap, and what you have to do to get the gold star. You emulate her, maybe even get a crush on her; after all, she brings order to chaos. If little Francois over there decides to take your crayon, pull your hair, or call you a bad word, all you have to do is let her know and she takes care of it. Better yet, she *knows* stuff, man. She's happy to tell you the answers to the millions of questions you have. She can read and write and do all those other things you see your parents doing, and her whole job is to let you in on the secrets so you too can master those I'm-all-grown-up-and-can-do-it-by-myself skills. Pretty soon you find yourself a willing deputy, happy to shout out any time you see a rule being broken. She is cool, and really not that much older than you are (nothing like the inconceivable age your parents have achieved). All you gotta do is be like her and you too can be cool. The consequence: lesson one is firmly fixed forever in your mind—*the secret to happiness is <u>external</u>; please "them" and everything will be all right.*

Grades as Gods

Next, somewhere along the line you are introduced to the wonderful world of grades. Ah grades—what would school be without them? They are our first formal

---

[5] Let's assume it's a "she"…how many of us had men as kindergarten teachers? Of course, that's a subject for another whole book.

introduction to being rated.[6] Grades come to define everything about the school experience from the classes we are allowed to take to our choice of colleges. We even invent a social status around grades. In my day there were the "brains" at one end of the scale who were in the "advanced classes," and the "burn outs" at the other end who sometimes didn't even make it to class. Everyone else was just average, so ordinary they didn't even merit a label. And we had it easy when I was in school. Nowadays, grades are more than just a comment on us, they are a comment on our whole school. Botch that State Standardized Test designed to bring Accountability Into The System, and you've not only failed yourself but also your school and your community. Scarlet letter, anyone?

That said, grades are essential. As I stated in the last chapter, results *are* important. I fully support the quest for results. In fact, I *welcome* being graded on my performance. Measuring performance is a good thing. We must know where we stand. How else can we improve? You can't stick your head in the sand and expect the rest of the world to pamper you. Aggression and competition are not bad things; they help us make a better world. They can even be a lot of fun if you handle them the right way. Anyone who has been an athlete can attest to the pure joy of competition. Yes it's nice to win, but it's way more fun to be part of a great, closely contested match than to win a boring, one-sided game.

The bad thing about grades isn't what they are, it's what we've done with them. We've turned them into a kind of

---

[6] ...that is, unless you have really ambitious parents who enroll you in soccer at age 2 ½ and scream at you, the coach, and everyone within shouting distance when your team loses.

religion. They have come to define what success is supposed to be; they are the definition of what is "good." Even the language surrounding them reinforces this: an "A" is "excellent," a "B" is "good," "C" is "average," "D" is "below average" and, the worst of all, "F" for *failure*." Rather than a benchmark telling us where we are on the path to a goal, *they become the goal*. The grade is all.

Consequently, we learn to game the system to get that grade above and beyond all else. How many of us have "crammed" for a test? Yeah, there's some high quality learning for you. How many of us can think back to a class where we got "an A" but now don't remember a single thing we "learned" from that class? But hey, no worries…it's OK! We did the important thing: we got the grade, which got us into college, which got us the chance to get more grades, which got us a whole diploma's worth of grades, which got us into our job working for a whole new grading system (now it's called "performance reviews") so we can happily keep chasing the grade until we keel over from exhaustion.

The result of all this grade mania is a second lesson firmly fixed in our minds—that *success is pre-defined for us by someone else*. Do not pass GO, do not use your own imagination. The whole game is to look outside yourself, for someone else to tell you exactly what you should be doing, and then do what they say better than the next guy can do it. All we have to do is get "them" to tell us what "it" is, and then "make the grade." Put that with lesson one and what you have is the following: not only is our focus external (versus internal), but we also have come to expect that success comes in pre-packaged, color-by-number recipes (versus something to be discovered) and is defined for us by others who are wiser than we.

Every Man is an Island

Tighten your seat belt because there's one more little jewel of a lesson that we learn as we go along, perhaps the worst of the lot: *you are on your own.* Grades are an individual measure of your performance relative to everyone else. They are there to separate the "smart" people from the "dumb" people. What if you are in a class of all smart people? Not to worry, "ve hav vays of separating za men from za boys." If all else fails, we'll use a curve. That way, by definition, we will be guaranteed to get whatever profile of performance we want, regardless of the actual skills of the individuals in the class. No need to do anything reasonable like, oh, setting an objective standard and motivating as many students as possible to meet that standard. Just curve it, and you'll be guaranteed to get a nice, standard distribution of performance no matter how lousy of a teacher you are. Of course there some undesirable side effects such as the student who misses one small point on a test which is the difference between and "A" (good) and a "B" (nice try, but you really aren't up there with the best). But hey, at least we got what we wanted and were able to affix labels to everyone in the class.

Above all, we have made sure everyone understands lesson three loud and clear: *it's every man for himself.* Every man is an island. Don't look for anyone to help you, and don't be so quick to give away your advantage by helping someone else either. Well, OK, if you have to do something about those terrible urges you have to help others, you can tutor someone in another class. But you had better not even think about working with someone in your own class. We have a special and very bad label for that kind of activity: *cheating.*

By the time you finish college you have become a expert caretaker of this three-headed monster. Everything about you is tuned to providing what they want, according to the rules they define, and doing it largely by yourself. You are an island, kept weak by isolation because to talk about it with someone else would be cheating. All your attention is focused externally; you are still pleasing *them*. You can't even pick what success means for you; instead, you characterize success in terms others define for you and spoon feed to you. And everyone around you helps reinforce this spoon feeding through peer pressure as they choke down their own dose of the same medicine. You are the perfect free-market prey, empty of any goals except those set for you on TV, ready—no, eager—to be told what to do and who to be so you can hurry up and get to it. You are twenty-two years old, educated out the wahzoo, programmed to do whatever they tell you to give them what they want.

Nowhere along the way did we teach you how to ask what *you* want. Nowhere did we teach you how to use rules, grades, and self-reliance to power your own definition of success.

Belief systems like this are incredibly strong. They are so much a part of everything and everybody you almost can't see they are there. They are literally ingrained, since your earliest days, and become such a fundamental assumption you can't separate them from reality. You don't see them for the arbitrary thing they are. They are like a bad smell that you got used to so long ago you don't even notice the stink any more. And before you know it, you find yourself staying late at the office just because a coworker does (huh?), or you find yourself running ragged trying to make sure everyone else in the house is happy before you give yourself even a moment's rest (what?), or you find yourself shelling out an extra $20K for that Ford Land Walrus SUV because...because...well, because a Super Bowl commercial said you would be a dork if you drove anything else. *They told you to*, and a good student does what they say.

Aaaah! Enough already; I can't write anymore or I'll get too depressed. How do we break out of all this? We've already said you need grades because they help you assess your skills so you can get where you want to go. Also, you must also have rules to keep some kind of order in a society. And being self-reliant and able to drawn upon your own resources when you have to is clearly an advantage. I mean, what else is there, some kind of giant welfare state? Getting rid of all rules, grades, and self-reliance would be like endorsing communism, and we all know how well *that* system worked out. So rules, grading, and self-reliance are here to stay, yet we've just shown how being too obsessed about them can paint us into a very unhappy corner. It all sounds like a catch-22.

That's where *blame* comes in; or rather, the *lack* of blame. The whole key is to drive blame completely out of your life. Ironically enough, the way to do that is to embrace blame in a way that allows you to harness its power to drive your own agenda.

Turning the Tables

First, you must realize that nobody is at fault here. There is nothing wrong with being graded and nobody made a mistake teaching you that it is important to be able to compete. You *had* to be shown the rules of the game. Someone had to set boundaries for when you were young so you would learn that you can't just run amok in the world. There a lot of things we have to share in this world, like the roads, and if we don't all agree to the rules the system would never work. If I just arbitrarily decided to drive on the wrong side of the road I'd probably kill somebody. Moreover, you need examples of rule setting so you can learn to make your own rules when you need them, like limiting your spending so your life isn't in the hands of some credit card company, or cutting your food intake to keep your weight down. And as we've said now multiple times, we live in a market-based world where you will be judged—and you will judge others—based on performance. Knowing the rules, how to stick to them, and how you rate compared to others is absolutely fundamental. Your kindergarten teacher would have been remiss had she not taught you about rules and held you too them.

So nobody is to blame. Not your kindergarten teacher, not your Mom, not your Dad, not even your high school English teacher who made you memorize the prolog to Chaucer's *The Canterbury Tales* in the original Old English.[7] Most importantly, *you are not to blame.* You did what you had to do, and it was right at the time. So stop kicking yourself over your past. Forget about any mistakes you may have made along the way. Let them go. OK, learn from them so you don't make the same mistakes, but let them go. Dwelling on blame doesn't do anything for anyone. Ever. Period. Blaming never, ever, *ever*, helps you out. Never. Have I made my point yet? Blame just saps your energy and keeps you from making progress.

---

[7] Some "learning" sticks no matter how hard you try to reuse that part of your own internal hard disk—I can *still* recite that silly prolog.

Once you open the door to a blame-free life it's like dropping a 70 pound pack you've been carrying around for years. If you really want to see this in your own life, take the challenge my mentor gave to me: *try living your life completely without blame of any sort*. Sound easy? Heh...just wait until you give it a try. You will be amazed by how much blame we all practice simply as a matter of habit.

Step 1: Take a Blame Inventory

Here's how to get started. First, get yourself a small pad and pencil that you can carry around with you (or the electronic equivalent). Every time you find yourself saying "I can't," write it down. Now, there are many ways that we tell ourselves "I can't." Sometimes it's "I can't do such-and-such because..." Sometimes it's "I can't enjoy myself when I am doing such-and-such (e.g., commuting to work) because..." Sometimes it's "I can't stand it when..." As a signal to alert you to when you are into blame, you can use your own anger, frustration, or excuses. When you find yourself getting angry, agitated, cynical, upset or offering an excuse, it is a sign of blame. Did that guy who cut you off on the road piss you off? Blame. Find yourself saying that you can't get something done at work because of some stupid co-worker? Blame. Wishing you were taller, shorter, thinner, or had better hair so others would find you more attractive? Blame. Find yourself saying "things would be better if only ..."? Blame.

We fill our lives with blame statements. Why? Because we have our "grade hats" on. Remember, we are comfortable being graded and have been conditioned to automatically rate ourselves against others. Our whole culture reinforces this, pelting us night and day with signals about how we are "inadequate." In that kind of environment, blaming becomes almost a matter of sanity; if we don't find ways of blaming someone or something outside of ourselves, our self esteem gets ground to a pulp. That is, unless, we find a way out of the trap, using principles like the ones in this book.

If you actually play this little accounting game (I call it the blame game) with yourself, you will be astounded at how many times you find yourself making an excuse for one thing or another. I was mortified at how often I did. It almost got sickening. Nearly one out of every three thoughts in my head was about some obstacle or another that was "preventing" me from doing the things I really wanted to do. I couldn't believe it.

More importantly, it opened my eyes to the shocking amount of time and energy I was spending on something that turns out to be completely pointless: *blaming someone or something else accomplishes absolutely nothing.* I can sling blame with the best of them, but after all the dust settles and I've finally tired myself out *I'm still right where I was before I launched into the blame game.* Actually, that's not true; I'm right where I was plus I've wasted precious time and energy that I can never get back. Worst of all, I'm no closer to being where I want to be.

However, take heart. This cloud has a silver lining. Having kept a blame inventory will help you build an awareness that is the key to turning the tables in your favor.

Step 2: Use Blame as Your Compass

Once you've played the blame game for about a month or so, you will have a feel for how often, and in what circumstances, you lean on blame to keep yourself right where you are. It will become an alarm of sorts, like a sixth sense. You'll be able to say "oh yea, that's just me blaming all the other drivers on the road for why I can't have fun on my commute to work" or "yep, there I go again blaming my boss for why I'm unhappy at my job" or "ho hum, that's me again blaming my kids for why my spouse and I can't have more romance in our lives."

And then an interesting thing will begin to happen. As you consciously acknowledge your blame statements, you will also uncover your own deepest desires. You'll begin to—dare I say it—tap in to your own *internal* wishes and needs. You will begin to sense patterns that reveal the things you want to change because you will see how much time you spend thinking about them. And at that point, the great irony of blame will reveal itself to you. Sure, blame is a negative thought, but the fact that you are dwelling on a topic can be turned into a positive. After all, *if you are spending that much time and energy on something, it must be important to you.* If it weren't, you wouldn't care.

The truth is we simply don't assign blame for things we don't care about. We don't blame the sun for rising in the east and setting in the west. We don't blame the sky for being blue or the grass for being green. That would be ludicrous. However, it might not be too much of a stretch to find yourself blaming the trees for dropping leaves all over your lawn which your wife then nags you to rake up on Saturday instead of watching that game on TV. Or, instead of blaming the tree, perhaps you blame your wife for being a nag, or your neighbor for planting that behemoth tree so close to your property, or the builders who laid out your neighborhood for putting the houses so close together, or the whole concept of suburban living that makes you feel like you need a leaf-free front yard. In the end, it really doesn't matter who or what you blame. The blame is a diversion, a symptom of something else. It's a side effect, a reflection of the real desires underneath. But since you've never been taught to listen to your real desires, out comes the blame and there it ends.

When you think of blame as a signal, it becomes an asset. It's a doorway to your own dreams. Maybe the reason those damn leaves piss you off so much really has *nothing to do with the leaves.* Maybe you just hate yard work, despite the fact that, as a "real man," you are *supposed* to like yard tools. Watch any gardening show and the commercials will make you think every red blooded guy in the world wants nothing more than to jump out of bed early on Saturday so he can zoom around his yard on a riding mower. Maybe you really never wanted to live in the suburbs and would rather not have a yard at all. The city might be the place for you, in a high-rise condo down town. But you have kids and if you have kids then you are supposed to want to live in the suburbs, right? Or perhaps you are neutral on the whole subject, and what you really want is to take time for yourself on Saturday after putting in a full week's worth of work, but you feel guilty asking your family to give you a couple of free hours on the weekend so you can pamper yourself. After all, a good dad (or mom) has to make sure everyone else is happy first, right?

See what I mean? *We don't blame if we don't care.* Blame is a mask; strip it away and you will find what you really want lying beneath. And that is the secret to getting rid of blame altogether. Once you can sense yourself drowning in blame, you can throw yourself a life jacket by thinking about what you really want to do that the blame is hiding. And that's when you can start taking the "I can't" junk out of your life and start substituting "I want" instead.

Step 3: Revenge of the Kindergartener

This is where it gets fun. You've played the blame game and done an accounting. You've found a few areas where you seem to be blaming everything that moves. Now, you can take those three deadly lessons you learned in kindergarten and turn them to your advantage. Consider it the final lesson, the one you were never taught, showing you how to use those three terrible lessons (terrible until now) as fuel to drive *your* engine so you can start doing what *you* want for a change.

First, embrace the blame. Use it like a failing grade, a big fat "F" telling you that you need a wake up call. But think "F" for "focus" rather than for "failure." Or even "F" for "you know what, I'm sick and tired of getting my butt kicked and I'm ready to start having some *F-U-N*." For example, you're tired of your weekends being one chore after another; you want to figure out some way to do something for yourself.

OK, you've identified something you want to do or change…now what? Well, think of it this way: the blame has identified an undesirable state. You are "here" and you want to get "there." Instead of continuing to say "I can't" (blame) start saying "I want" instead. You are in an unhappy state, you've been uncomfortable about it at some level, and you have been running around blaming everything and everyone else so you can hide from that discomfort. Every time you feel yourself saying "I can't," take the time to pause and ask yourself instead "what do *I* really want?" I mean literally take the time to pause; I've had days when I've been on the road, driving like a jerk, mad at everyone else who is "driving the wrong way," and I've literally pulled off the road to take 5 minutes to ask "what the heck is really bugging me?"

That will help you get underneath the blame, and you will be ready to make a change. Don't worry if it takes you a while to figure out exactly what the blame is hiding; just go with whatever strikes you as the right direction. If you get it wrong, you can rest assured your old blame habits will resurface, and then you can try another direction (remember, process, not result).

Next, you will need a plan. You will need a mechanism that will enable you to build a process that will propel you from where you are to where you want to be. Guess what? You can turn back to the same three lessons you learned in school: the rules, the grades, and the self-reliance. Those same three lessons that led to destructive thinking in the first place can be leveraged to create a process for self-driven change.

Upgrade Your Grading System

First, the grades. You know how to rank things and you can rank yourself here as well. In fact, you have already been doing that ranking; it is what has caused the blame to bubble up. But this time, you do your grading with a twist—instead of using an external measure of the grade, use *your own internal* measure. What you will be doing, effectively, is keeping your own feet to the fire, grounding yourself in reality by checking your progress against a goal you have set. The grade is still an absolute measure, like how much weight you have lost, but it is relative to an *internal* goal *you* have set, versus some external standard set by "them."

And that makes all the difference in the world, because you will be taking charge of your life. You will be the one setting the standard. You can start as big or as small as you like. There is no "right" answer. So, for example, you can say "you know, I want to lose 10 pounds." That's it, just 10 pounds. Not "I have to be like a super model on the cover of those ridiculous magazines at the grocery store." Rather, it's a personal goal, like "I want to spend at least 1 night a week out with my spouse" or "I want to have more fun on my commute to work" or "I want to exercise every day" or "I want to spend two hours every weekend doing something just for fun" or whatever. It is your goal, defined by you. Only now, you use the grading system we were all taught to hold your own feet to the fire, not because you are trying to please *them* but because you are trying to please *you*.

Rewrite Your Rules

Next come the rules. You start making a structure for yourself by inventing whatever rules you think you need to achieve your goal. These rules become *your* process, the mechanism you will use to make progress. Follow the rules and you are winning, regardless of when the end goal is reached. For instance, you might announce that you'd like to try making every Saturday morning from 8:00 to 10:00 "Dad time," test it for a few weeks, and see whether it works out. Will you get it right on the first try? Probably not. So what? Keep grading yourself and comparing the results against the goal you are trying to reach—but remember to stay focused on process, not results. Reward yourself if you are following the rules you have set for yourself to reach your goal. If you are seeing progress, then you have hit on a good rule. If not, you have eliminated a candidate rule; toss it out and try another one.

Where do these rules come from? From you. They are internal rules that you create to govern your own behavior. Maybe they are borrowed from friends, or even from books like this that give you suggestions. Perhaps they even come from breaking a "rule," like deciding you are going to walk your dog while you take that conference call instead of just sitting at your desk. The details of the rules don't matter as much as your willingness to actively seek out and set rules for yourself and then stick to them.

Summon Up Your Self-reliance

Sticking to your rules is where you fall back upon self-reliance. Remember having to work by yourself to get all those grades in school? Remember how sometimes it felt so lonely having to study for a test, so frightening to have to do it by yourself, yet you still stepped up to face that fear? Eventually, you were able to get through. And even if you weren't a whiz at school, or even never finished school, you've done plenty of other things that were hard where you had no choice but to rely upon yourself. Maybe you've raised kids (or are currently raising kids), perhaps even as a single parent. Maybe you've overcome a tough divorce. Maybe you've gone without a high school or college degree and still made a living. Maybe you've started your own business. Maybe you've been able to find yourself new jobs after getting laid off. Who knows. No matter what the circumstances, I guarantee you that you've had to tap into self-reliance. If nothing else, you've been self-reliant enough to keep yourself going, and in this fast-paced and ever-changing world that is no small feat. You've proven your self-reliance, even if not in the traditional ways, and now you can draw upon that strength again. But this time the rules are set by *you*, and the grading is done by *you*, to achieve a goal that is important to *you*.

Others will scoff, of course. In fact, you should *count on it*. That's why your self-reliance will be so important. Your neighbor down the street who is overweight will not want to see you losing weight because that will push his blame buttons. Your parents who never made it through school might say you are getting too big for your britches by thinking you can get a college degree. That guy driving the Hummer will laugh at your decision to save money by buying a fuel-efficient Saturn instead. Your friends who are more interested in wallowing in their own "I can't" statements won't be too happy hearing you say "I can." At least, not at first and not on the outside. So expect the ridicule. Look for it. It will be a sure sign you are on the right track. When I want to make a change in my life, I get nervous if I don't hear at least one person close to me tell me I'm crazy.

So you will need your self-reliance to keep you going. What did you expect? As my mentor is fond of saying, "if you always do what you've always done, you'll always get what you've always got." The whole culture is beating the same drum. The peer pressure to be like everyone else will raise its ugly head. Why are two-thirds of Americans overweight? Why do Americans work insane numbers of hours? Why do so many people have a Jacuzzi in their home they rarely use? Why are we all driving around in huge, gas guzzling SUVs? Peer pressure will be there, my friend.

However, remember this. You aren't seeking change for change's sake. You aren't out to put anyone else down for being overweight, or for driving a big car, or for working long hours. Other folks may have perfectly good reasons for doing those things. In truth, you aren't motivated by anything external *at all*. You are simply pursuing an internal goal that you have realized is important to you, *without judgment or blame for yourself or for anyone else*. You are simply trying to celebrate your life, and your own ability to take what you have and make something better, and have some fun while you are doing it.[8]

And when you get in that blame-free mind set, a wonderful thing happens. You feel good about yourself regardless of everyone else. You feel happy about your life in ways you haven't felt for a long time. You feel in control because *you* are deciding what is important, *you* are setting the rules, and you can feel great simply because you are sticking to those rules. That kind of attitude is highly contagious. It will build on itself inside of you and it will be reflected to those around you. Along the way, you will find that *you have become an inspiration to the real friends that surround you*. Some, who may have initially scoffed, you may find coming back to you at the oddest moments and saying "you know, I gotta say that I respect what you have been able to do. Can you give me a few pointers?" And of course you will be glad to lend a hand, bursting at your seams to share your insights on a process that you know will help someone else improve their own life. It will give you a renewed strength and energy unlike anything you've felt.

Rules, grades, self-reliance. We learned them well, but with an external focus in mind. Turn them inward and they are tools for redefining our lives. Blame is the key that

---

[8] You are, in fact, following the "Rule of Judgment," see pg 134.

unlocks the door. Stop saying "I can't" and start saying "I want" instead. Invent your own rules to pursue your own goals. Grade your own progress. And stick to your guns; it's your life and you only go around once. After all, how long did you plan on letting "them" run your life?

Story: With the Right Shades

This is a story about a picture that hangs on the wall in my office. It's a poster actually; a movie poster that has had some of its elements switched around to make a clever pun. The story of how this poster came to be made is a perfect example of the power of living completely without blame.

First, you need some background. As I said earlier, I work in a job that runs multiple innovation projects a year. We seek out new ideas that are percolating inside the company and assemble the equivalent of S.W.A.T. teams to take those ideas and see how far they can be pushed in an intensive, 12-week period. It's a lot of work, especially for the teams that devote themselves to seeing whether they can take these ideas and turn them into a new market for the company. But we also like to keep it fun, both to help the teams blow off steam and also to provide that extra cultural edge that brings the teams closer together and helps them achieve things they might not otherwise accomplish in a more traditional environment.

As part of the fun, we schedule a big "show-and-tell" event for the end of the 12-week session. And it is an event. We put on a show, giving each of the teams a chance to present to some of the highest executives at the company. We have both a formal presentation as well as a demo room, much like a trade show, where each team has a booth where they can show the fruits of their labor.

And to give it all a kind of pseudo Hollywood atmosphere, we encourage the teams to make movie posters of their projects.

These movie posters are a ton of fun. It's for a completely internal audience, so the teams will often download popular movie posters from the Internet and tweak them. It's not uncommon to see a familiar poster with the faces or names changed, or the wording changed to make a pun on the name of the project. It's all in the spirit of fun, and it makes the show much more interesting for both the participants and the audience. We have a hallway between the room where we give the formal presentations and the demo room, and we line the whole corridor with these posters. It always draws positive comments from the audience.

Last year, I was defining a new set of messages for our whole program. In this new set of messages, we refer to each of our different programs as a different "shade" of the original program. I had been working on the idea a long time and it was important. We were struggling to take several different programs, which on the surface all seemed different, and weave them into a consistent story. When we finally came up with the "shades" idea it was like breathing a huge sigh of relief. We'd finally hit on an image that would be easy to understand and communicate. Unfortunately, it was the night before our big show-and-tell event. To be specific, I had 40 minutes before the deadline for overnight shipping of anything we needed to have at the event.

That was when my boss hit me with the following: "Paul, this shades idea is great. Let's present this at the show-and-tell event. And by the way, you should probably create a movie poster for this as well so it will look as cool as everything else."

Uh...pardon me? A movie poster? *IN 40 MINUTES*?

I hung up the phone a bit stunned. It was one of those whiplash moments; you know, when something clicks after a long effort, you share the results, you get great feedback, and then you get hit with an immediate follow on action. I recall literally laughing out loud; the idea of getting a movie poster together in less than 40 minutes was beyond absurd. It typically took us weeks to produce a good poster. My brain instantly went into blame mode. There wasn't enough time. I didn't have the creative skills it would take to come up with a cool poster. I didn't know any of the software used to doctor up a movie poster, even if I could find one. I had no idea where to search on the Internet to even find a movie poster, even if an idea did occur to me. There was, in fact, such a long line of circumstances that I could blame, so many obstacles I could readily put in my own way, that it made me laugh, albeit with a slightly hysterical edge.

I could easily have just said "no way" and gone home. It was late after all, and the deadline was so short, nobody would have blamed me (see the blame again?) if I didn't come up with a poster. But for some reason, I took a different tack. I said to myself, "well why not? What do I have to lose?" To this day, I still don't know what got into me. It may have been the fact that the deadline was so absurdly short that it provided me with a kind of weird freedom. I literally had nothing to lose and there was no way in anyone's wildest dreams that I would actually succeed in producing a poster. The expectations were so outrageous they became immaterial. The "grade" disappeared. The "standard rules" didn't apply. I had 40 minutes to burn; why not see how far I could run with this thing?

So I put my feet up and got thinking about shades. Shades...hmmm. It sounded like sun glasses. I went into the lab and started tossing ideas around with a co-worker. Rose colored glasses. Innovation. What about a pun on some movie poster with sun glasses? We could turn them blue, as in IBM blue, and make a pun on the shades. So, what movie poster has sun glasses in it? Ding...the *Risky Business* movie. Heck, sun glasses were one of the main props of that movie and it was definitely a cool movie poster. We had spent 10 minutes.

From there, we started moving around the lab, asking various people for help. Who knows which web sites have movie posters? Can you search for something for me? Which version of the poster is in a format we can modify? Which has the best resolution? Who knows how to run the software to modify the image? Ah, you do...great, can you change these sun glasses to have blue lenses? Meanwhile, I'll work on the wording...maybe something along the lines of how innovation is "risky business" unless you are looking at it through the "right shade of blue." Yeah, that will work. Can you match that font with this new sentence? Great, that looks perfect. Let's print it an ship it. We had spent a total of 38 minutes.

That story never ceases to amaze me. I keep the poster on my wall for a couple of reasons. First, it's an eye catcher, and when people walk by they almost always ask "so tell me about the shades." It does exactly what I wanted it to do—it gets people engaged in our program in ways that a boring, dry presentation never could. But the poster also has a secret meaning for me that gets reinforced every time I walk in my office. It's the ultimate example of the power of giving up blame. Look at what I was able to do *simply by shifting my perspective.* Instead of spending time telling myself how many problems were in my path, I just threw myself into the job without expectations. I took the perspective of "let's have fun and see what happens." In fact, when you think about it, I accidentally did something very profound—I changed my paradigm of expectations. It wasn't as though I had no expectations, just not the ones I typically have. Instead of expecting results or expecting a particular performance, I expected to have fun and see what I could get done. That kind of liberating attitude left me wide open to do what I could, to tap into my abilities in a completely unburdened way. It also gave me the freedom to concentrate on what I was good at (the play on words) and seek out others to fill in where my skills were weak. It allowed me to drop the baggage of blame and "dance as if nobody was watching." I achieved the impossible because I gave up blame, played to my strengths, let others help me, and concentrated on just being myself. *That's* the way I try to live every moment.

Story: The Parent Nanny

I've claimed that belief systems are powerful things, so insidious that we often can't see them for the arbitrary things they are. This was never so evident to me than with the following story about our "Parent Nanny." The amazing thing about this story is that it continues to unfold this day. I still run into people who, when I relate the story, look at me like I've shown them they always had wings and could fly but they just never noticed.

The story starts after Kathryn (my wife) and I had our first child. Fast forward a bit to when we have our second child, let the tape run a bit more, then slow back down to normal speed when the kids hit the age when they can go to day care. Zoom in on the daily routine and watch the following episode of how life was for us on a regular basis, as two working parents trying to do our jobs and raise our kids.

Things would get started around 5:30 am, a difficult time for me as I am definitely not a morning person. But with kids, deciding whether or not you are going to be a morning person isn't an option, plus there is so much to get done you really need the extra hours in the morning to get everyone ready for their day. We had chosen the day care route at this point versus a dedicated stay-at-home nanny or parent. We both like to work, so having one of us as a stay-at-home mom or dad didn't work. In considering full-time care, we rejected the idea of a nanny in favor of day care because we felt that the socialization with other children would be a positive benefit for our kids. We'd found an absolutely wonderful day care and our eldest had been attending for a year with great results. So there was nothing at all negative about our situation; we were happy with our choice and really just needed to figure out the mechanics of how to make it all work.

That's where the difficulty came in. As anyone who has children or elderly parents or any other kind of dependent can tell you, you don't have a waking minute to spare. Our day would start off with chores and end with chores. In between, there were more chores to do. What about weekends? More of the same—caring for dependents doesn't include "time off". That's the thing about a dependent; dependency is a 24x7 kind of thing. From the moment we got up we'd get right in to the routine: getting everyone up, getting everyone fed, getting everyone dressed, getting everyone's stuff packed up, getting everyone to their destination. And typically this meant a longer commute which meant that there was no time to spare at work. No more time for breaks because you either had to come in bit late after dropping off at day care or you had to leave a bit early to pick up.

The pace didn't slacken when we got home for the evening. There was dinner to cook, stuff to unpack, pets to take care of, clothes to get into the wash. And we both wanted to actually spend time with our kids as well; after all, that's why we wanted to be parents in the first place. I *like* my kids and I *want* to spend time with them. Invariably they would come home with some new art project or science experiment, or maybe we'd just sit and do a puzzle together. You can't pass that stuff up; kids grow up way too quickly and get so busy with their own friends that you only really get a few years to bond with them as young children. But of course all of this meant that things like dinner, laundry, or leisure time for Mom and Dad got pushed way to the back burner.

Hence, optimization became the driving principle of our lives. We tried everything to cut down on the amount of time we needed for chores like dishes, laundry, yard work, etc. We bought microwave dinners, paper plates, and plastic forks and spoons. We bought placemats that would catch most of what scattered off little plates at the dinner table. We packed our own lunches to try to squeeze more out of each day at work. We hired someone to do our lawn work, and actively ignored how much the bushes were getting overgrown.

But in the end, nothing really worked. The evenings were the worst, probably because that's when fatigue was the biggest factor. Kathryn and I would arrive home with neither of us having spent even 5 minutes thinking about dinner. That meant most of the time we'd get the kids something to eat and ignore ourselves. "You've got to take time to eat healthy" we'd tell them as we grabbed a snack on the fly to keep from keeling over. We never ate together as a family, which bugged me. After dinner, we focused on spending time with our kids, goofing off until bed time when we headed upstairs for the bath-then-brush-your-teeth-then-read-me-a-story-then-sit-and-talk-with-me-then-tuck-me-in routine. By then it was close to 9 pm, and Kathryn and I would head downstairs to cook *our* dinner, which mostly consisted of "what's in the freezer that I can I throw in the micro?" kind of cuisine. Oh yeah...super healthy. And then came the final act, The Big Cleanup, which really amounted to trying to keep enough of the things like dishes, laundry and general picking up at bay so we wouldn't be completely overwhelmed the next day, when we had to do it all over again. After that it was "Oh, yeah, hi honey. How was your day anyway? Sorry for the yawn, I really am interested...really...I'm just so tired. Guess maybe we'll talk tomorrow sometime, but sheesh we gotta hit the sack because the alarm goes off at 5:30."

Of course, this was completely unsustainable, even for a type-A, I-can-do-it-by-myself, kinda guy like me. That's when Kathryn had her flash of brilliance, one evening, in a conversation that went something like this:

"Why not hire a nanny for *us*?" she suggested.

"Huh? What are you talking about? I thought we agreed on day care?"

"No, a nanny for us. For you and me."

"But I *want* to be with the kids. I don't want to pay for someone to come in and take care of the kids. *I* want to do that."

"No, Paul, you are completely missing my point. I'm not talking about a typical nanny. I'm not talking about someone who would come in to watch the kids. I want to be with the kids too. I like it. What I'm talking about is someone to come in and do all the chores we hate doing, so we can be with the kids."

"So, kinda like a cook or a housekeeper…"

"Well, sort of, but really 'nanny' fits better if you think of this person as someone looking after *us*. Put it this way: I'm suggesting we *outsource* the evening chores to someone else so we can spend our evenings focusing on what we really want to do."

"OH! So you mean, like, a nanny for you and me."

"Yes," she said, smiling, "that's what I said ten minutes ago."

"Right, well," I said, smiling sheepishly, "I do have a college degree, but I can still be educated. It just takes longer."

The next day, I was on the internet, surfing the University of Texas web site (our local university). We had a local labor pool perfectly suited to the kind of job we were offering: show up around 5:00 pm, maybe pick up the kids from school, cook dinner, get a free meal, and you're all done by 8:00. If college today is anything like it was for me, things aren't even getting ramped up until 8:00 pm. And a free meal for a college student, heck that's like waving a red flag in front of a bull. Within a few days, I had taken out the following ad at "hire-a-longhorn.org":

WANTED: "Parent Nanny" (part-time household assistant & cook for family of 4)

Duties: Cooking meals, cleaning up after dinner, emptying dishwasher, making kids' meals, occasional light grocery shopping (if we run out of something), neaten house (note: not maid work).

Typical Day: show up at 5:00, cook dinner, stay for dinner (welcome to join us), clean up after dinner, make kids' lunches for the next day, neaten up house before leaving around 8:00.

Hours: 2-3 hours a day, 4 days a week. Fridays and weekends off. Option for extra days or babysitting if desired.

Other Requirements/Information:
- Must supply your own transportation
- No smokers
- We have a cat (if you have allergies)

We got 8 responses in the first day and within a week had hired someone.

It was like seeing the sunshine after a long dark storm. We now come home to a completely different life in the evenings. I come home and chat with my wife and play with my kids until I'm told dinner is ready. After dinner, I get up and play with the kids again until it's time for bath. We head up, give the kids a bath and read them stories. When we come downstairs around 9, the dinner dishes have been cleared, the house is neat, and the lunches for the next day are made. And best of all, Kathryn and I have time to spend on ourselves before we have to turn in for the night.

Now you would think this story would be easy to share with others. The amazing thing is how difficult it is convey. It's always the same kind of reaction. First, the blank puzzled look. Then the same kinds of questions: "You got a nanny? For your kids? Why on earth would you do that if you are paying for day care? So, what, she comes and takes care of the kids in the evening? Don't you ever spend time with your kids?" And then I have to explain it all a second time: "No, no! It's a nanny for *us*, for me and Kathryn. She comes and takes care of us so we can be with our kids. We outsourced the stuff we don't want to do, so we can focus on the things we like to do."

It just amazes me how people don't understand the concept when I first explain it. It's like there is this huge blind spot. For a long time it puzzled me why this was so, and why I got such a consistent, confused reaction. And then it hit me that Kathryn and I had gone against something so basic, so ingrained, that most people couldn't get their heads around it. We literally cannot imagine not doing all the boring chores of being a parent. That's what being a parent is. It's what a parent is "supposed" to do. It's what's *expected*. If you don't like it, you must either be unfit as a parent or it must mean either you or your spouse needs to quit work to stay at home. It is so much a part of our culture that *we never even think to question it*.[9]

Such a simple solution, yet it took Kathryn and me a long time to see it. I suspect there are a bunch of these sorts of conventions buried in our way of thinking. I wonder how many other things I think of as natural are actually holding me back. And if they are so much a part of us, and of everyone we know, do we have any hope of breaking free of their control?

---

[9] I say more about this in Chapter 4 when I cover the "walk through" ritual, a technique you can use to expose such deeply embedded "blind spots" (see pg 127).

I think yes, and I think that living without blame is the key. When I focus my attention on what I want to do, versus what I imagine I can't do (blame), it opens the door to challenging my assumptions. I aim for the goal and take my own desire as a given. The goal is never in question. Everything except the goal is negotiable, which opens me up to new possibilities. The actions I am taking are either contributing, or not contributing, to where I want to be. It's like solving a puzzle; you know the end result is possible, even if it all looks like a jumble at the beginning, because you can see the picture of the completed puzzle on the box. Work-life balancing is like that; give yourself a chance to believe in the end result and you will find a way to make it happen.

3 Embrace Your Passions

Principle 3: Find your passions in life and embrace them with every fiber of your being. If you do this, everything about your life will be easier, come faster, be healthier, take less time, and produce vastly more results. Nothing—absolutely nothing— can compete with passion.

The Strength of Ten

I love irony. You know, like those moments where you find yourself complaining about all the people who bitch at work, or when you yell at your kids for being rude, or when you bust your butt at a job you hate so one day you can have the good life. Life is full of irony, but when it comes to work-life balancing, nothing seems quite so ironic to me as the fact that I can actually get *more* done with *less* effort. It defies logic. Anyone claiming such a thing would surely be mad or, worse, must surely be trying to sell you something. It's a particularly sensitive point to make to someone struggling with work-life balancing because it is precisely what we all want to hear. Our lives are so full, so overwhelming, and we feel so "out gunned" all the time that any promise of more from less time draws us like moths to the flame. Yet I am here to tell you that you can indeed get more from less, far more than you believe possible. The key is passion and, once again, the secret to tapping into this magic lies completely within you.

Let's see if I can convince you that passion can give you a capability you don't have right now. Because that's what I am saying: that by tapping into passion you can get more done in less time. That implies there must be a *quantitative* difference in life for those following their passion versus those who do not. After all, there are still only 24 hours in a day. We aren't talking about a time warp here, and nobody is super human. You must still make allowances for sleep, vacation, relaxation, and just plain making mistakes. It follows, then, that there must be something else about passion that enables those who embrace it to somehow be more efficient or effective than the rest of us.

Reducing Your Overhead

Fundamentally, it's all about not working against yourself. To put it in business terms, it's like reducing overhead. If you reduce overhead, your business is more efficient and makes a higher profit. To put it in terms of physics, it's like reducing the friction in the system. If you take friction out of a system, it takes less energy to produce motion and you travel longer distances with each effort. So it is with passion. When you tap into your passion, it makes everything easier to start, simpler to maintain, and you produce better results.

To illustrate how passion reduces the friction in life, let's start by talking about the opposite: a life without passion. Think of all the extra friction there is in life when you feel listless or unmotivated. For example, getting up in the morning takes more time because you aren't excited about the day ahead. You lie in bed a little longer, you stumble down to make the coffee, you take an extra 5 minutes in the shower to pluck up the courage to face the day. You sit a few more minutes in the car listening to the end of that song before trudging across the parking lot to your building. Getting your work done is harder because you find you lack the motivation for why you are doing it. It takes longer to answer email, and you find yourself wasting time in repetitive arguments in meetings because you don't have a clear structure guiding your actions. All of this can lead to literally hours a day of wasted time.

The same kind of extra friction builds up in the social dimensions of your life as well, where you waste time worrying about what you ought to be doing or whether what you plan to do will be acceptable to those who are important in you life. For instance, being with your kids might feel like a chore. You might think "oh, God, what am I going to have to do to keep them happy now?" This is your family, and you know you need them or else you'd be alone. You can't risk pissing them off, right? You have to make sure you are sensitive to their needs, consequently all your interactions take on the form "if it's OK with you" or "that's fine, whatever you want to do." As another example, perhaps you are visiting your family, say at the holidays, and of course this is one of the few times you all actually get together, which means the time spent needs to be as perfect as it can be. And that means making sure you leave everyone feeling good about everyone else, which translates into everyone trying to guess what everyone else really wants, but isn't saying they want, so nobody will go home offended. Whaddya think, sound at all familiar? Or let's say you wake up on Saturday morning, wishing you could have slept in until noon. You start your day by asking your kids or your spouse or your significant other what they want. Not being stupid, they realize they have to think of something to reply, and that whatever they pick needs to be acceptable to you because, of course, they want to stay in your good graces too. So they try to guess what it is you want to hear, while you try to guess what it is they really want. And so on and so on, until everyone has wasted the entire morning trying to figure out what everyone else wants to do. Yikes…what a colossal waste of energy.

How much better would family get-togethers be if everyone were comfortable enough to say "hey, you know, I was thinking of doing this. Who's with me?" How much less time would be wasted on the weekends if everyone just took a moment to voice their expectations and then the family built a quick plan to work it all in? We've actually been trying this at my house on the weekends and it works great. We call it our "family meeting." We all get up whenever we get up and while we have breakfast we each talk about what we are looking forward to doing on the weekend. It can be anything, even just "hey I really wanted to sit and do nothing" is perfectly fine. We make no judgments about what anyone wants to do. There are only two rules: (1) you have to pick something you *want* to do, not that you feel you *need* to do, and (2) you have to be willing to cooperate so everybody gets to do at least one thing they want to do. It takes about 10 minutes tops, after which it's pretty obvious how the day needs to unfold. As an example, here's what happened last weekend. My five-year-old wanted to do was sit around, watch some TV and play computer games, and my older daughter wanted to go for a bike ride. I wanted to get in a run in the morning and my wife just wanted some quite time to read the paper. The morning, then, was obvious: I went for a ride with my older daughter as a warm up, after which we came back and I pushed her in one of those "zoom" strollers while I ran.

Meanwhile, my wife set up the computer for my younger daughter (with headphones, thank you very much) and then read the paper. Everybody was happy and it took almost no time to get organized. Instead of wasting hours feeling put out while we all pussy-foot around trying to read each others' minds, *we spent the bulk of our time actually doing what we all really wanted to do.*

And what about working at a job you feel excited about? Do you think it takes as much effort as a job you hate, or do you think being passionate about your work would lead to "reduced overhead" on the job? For instance, do you imagine it will take as long to get out of bed in the morning? No way—and I guarantee you that shower will be quicker as well. You'll probably find yourself getting the coffee ready to go the night before so you can get to work sooner. Emails will be much easier to answer because they will either apply to what you are excited about, in which case you will be able to rattle off a reply almost without thinking, or else they will be unrelated to your interests and you will quickly pass them off to someone else. Meetings will be much more productive for you as well, and you will find you won't feel "baited" into joining in on that same old tired argument that seems to come up every meeting. Sure, there will always be some uncooperative people to deal with, but you will find yourself automatically minimizing your time around them because you are drawn to other people who share your interests. In fact, when that same old tired topic comes up at the meeting, you may find yourself politely excusing yourself so you can go work on the fun stuff.

Instant Decision Making

When you carry your passions uppermost in your mind, it's like walking around with an automatic instant decision making box at your finger tips. You don't have to spend a lot of time planning because you can be confident you will do the right thing at the right time. You don't need to waste a lot of time building external structure because you have your own internal lighthouse. You don't have to predict what's going to happen because you know that whatever happens, it will be obvious whether or not it's something related to your interests. It will literally *feel* right. If it doesn't, you need only figure out how to either avoid it or, if it can't be avoided, then how to deal with it as efficiently as possible.

I'll give you a great example of how this happened to me this past year when my daughter started grade school. The move to the new school involved schedule changes, naturally, and I ended up taking on the task of having to be at the school at a specific time to pick her up. This was a new chore for me and, honestly, not something I wanted to do because it meant paying attention to the clock at the end of the day when I was used to being able to do my own thing. But I also had two passions I was pursuing at the time: I wanted to get more regular exercise and I also wanted to start spending more one-on-one time with each of my daughters. That's when I had the idea of moving my run to the end of the day, and timing it to start just long enough before when I had to pick up my daughter that I could finish my run at her school, pick her up, and spend some one-on-one time walking home with her. Thus a chore was turned into a way I could pursue two things I really wanted.

78

Now, I didn't have to wring my hands to figure this out. I did not sit down with some elaborate calendar and meticulously map out the details of my life. The solution just popped into my head. It was completely obvious *because I knew what I wanted* to be doing. I was thinking about how much I really wanted to run more consistently, and how much I wanted to spend time with my daughter, and wishing I didn't have the extra chore of having to be at a particular time and place and the end of each day. Put those three things together and anyone could devise the same solution I did. Now, do the teachers appreciate me showing up all sweaty? Not sure. Don't care, really. If they say something, I'll carry an extra towel or something, and mop the sweat from my receding hairline before heading into the school. And who knows, maybe they like looking at my legs (my hairline may be receding, but my vanity is intact).

The point is: embracing your passions gives you the power to eliminate most of life's decision making overhead. Decisions are simpler and can be made more quickly because it is so much easier to ignore the irrelevant. It's like going to a restaurant thinking, "you know, I think I want fish tonight." Just knowing that eliminates most of the menu from consideration. Compare that to thinking "I have no idea what I want to eat." Not knowing what you want means you'll take a whole lot longer to make up your mind.

Beyond a Doubt

There is another friction-reducing side effect of embracing your passions that is closely related to decision making: the reduction of doubt. How many times have you had to make a big decision and found yourself nervous about it? It might be a job change, getting married, or buying a house. Even something as straightforward as buying a car can do it; after signing on the dotted line and driving off the lot, you wake up the next day with that feeling of buyer's remorse. I'm talking about the time you spend chewing your nails after you have made you decision. You like that car and you've been wanting it for months. You fell in love with the house the first time you drove by. You know she's the right girl for you because she's the only one you've ever been around where you can feel completely at ease just being yourself. The new job is really exciting and you've been waiting for an opportunity like this to come along for a long time. But it's new, it's a risk, it's the unknown, and so doubt is part of the package. Doubt is another kind of overhead that chews up chunks of time without producing anything of value. It's not like you don't know what your decision has to be, you do; yet you worry about the consequences. It's not overhead spent making the decision, it's overhead spent dwelling upon a decision after you've made it.

Once again, passion provides the solution. It is the grease that will keep your gears moving even when doubt makes you feel like your engine is going to seize up. And there is one simple, compelling reason why. Despite all the feelings of doubt, despite the inescapable truth that you cannot know what lies ahead, you do have one rock solid certainty that you can take to the bank: *you know you will be doing something you enjoy.* No matter what else happens, you will be having a great time—by definition— because you will be pursuing the things you love to do the most. That certainty is your talisman to ward off doubt.

Think about it this way: if you were on your deathbed looking back at a life full of memories spent pursuing what you loved the most, how bad could that possibly be? You would know, *beyond a doubt*, that you had lived the best life you could have possibly lived no matter what had transpired. Given the information you had at the time, you took the chance and pursued what you wanted the most, and your steps were the lighter for it. By following your passion you are guaranteed to have a life full of experiences that are the most interesting to you. You may not ever know in advance exactly what those experiences will be, nor where things will lead; after all, much of life boils down to chance. You certainly won't always get precisely what you want. But you *will* get *the most* of what you want, and you will have a blast along the way. That much is guaranteed because you are following you passions which, by definition, are the things you like the most. Doubt is still there, but it plays a much smaller role. You don't need as much confidence in your actions because you have confidence you are following your heart, and any action taken in that direction is positive. You don't have to guess or predict or try to prepare for every contingency because you can know, in advance, that you will make the right decision whatever comes your way. How can you know this? Because you will be pursuing your passions; you will be making decisions to maximize your opportunity to do the things you like most.

If this sounds like circular reasoning, you're right. It is. That's part of the power of following your passions: you focus on what you really want to do, and doing what you like helps you keep your focus. It becomes a self-reinforcing way of living that helps you cut through all the B.S. in life that is always there, threatening to drain away you precious time and energy.

The Compounding Interest of Opportunity

If you're with me so far, then you have bought in to the idea that embracing passion will lead to less overhead, less overall stress in your life. You'll be doing what you want with a lot less fuss, and worrying about your decisions less. That's all well and good, and it does explain some of how passion will get you more with less, but it does not explain everything. How is it that some people seem to "have all the luck?" Reducing the friction in life is one thing, getting those dream opportunities is quite another. You might be saying, "OK, sure, I buy that passion will make things go easier for me, but that doesn't explain how I'm supposed to land those great opportunities I'm excited about in the first place. Explain that, Mr. smart guy." OK, then, I will. Here's my take on it: it amounts to what I call the "compounding interest" of opportunity.

The reasoning goes like this. You are looking to make a switch to something new. It can be anything; for instance, at the moment I am considering making a switch in my exercise routine to more cycling. I've never done it in my life. Don't know a thing about it. All I know is that after over 30 years of running on an almost continuous basis, my knees are ready for a break and I'm psyched about cycling as an alternative. Given cycling as a goal, I now have my "pointer" and I simply need to follow the series of opportunities that will unfold as I pursue it. It's like the six degrees of separation we have been told connect everyone together. It doesn't matter where you start because opportunities are all around us and one opportunity will naturally lead to another. *When you are pursuing a passion the opportunities compound* in a way that is extraordinarily powerful, the results of one opportunity making the next one exponentially simpler to come by. Before you know it, you will be turning opportunities away so you can get some sleep.

How does this work? It happens because passion is contagious. Simply put, people like it. Everyone wants to be around someone who is excited and who looks like they are having a good time. We are all emotional creatures. We do a good job of dressing things up with logic, but bottom line we are all emotional. We want to have fun, and nothing is more fun than being around people who are *genuinely* having a good time. I'm not talking about the phony stuff, I'm talking about the real thing, and we all know it when we see it. Even children, at a very young age, can sense when someone is giving them the straight scoop versus a pile of you-know-what. Guess what—those who are handing out the opportunities can sense it too. They know who is really excited about their job versus who is just brown-nosing. They have to pick people to manage and to live with while they pursue their own goals. What kind of people do you think managers prefer to be around? Some companies, like IBM, go so far as to make it explicit, practically hitting us over the head to encourage us to pursue our passions. IBM has published a series of "leadership qualities" which the company states it is looking for in its leaders. And right up there at the top, IBM says it is looking for, and I quote, "those with a *passion* for the business." IBM is all but coming right out and saying that the best opportunities will go to those who follow their passions.

Opportunity, *when you are pursuing your passion*, leads to more and greater opportunity. Volunteer to lend a hand on something that excites you and soon people will notice and give you more to do. You'll be reliable because you will be eager to do the work. You'll work more efficiently because of all the reduced overhead we talked about earlier. The result: you will succeed and people will notice. You will become a "go-to" person, someone people remember. And when that next opportunity comes along, you will find you are on the short list. Remember that saying "be careful what you wish for because you just might get it?" They were talking about passion. Show the world our passion and it will throw opportunities your way as fast as you want to take them on.

As I write this, it has been two weeks since my decision to start cycling. In that time, I've talked with a couple of friends who have introduced me to others who can advise me on how to select a bike. I've got a time slot scheduled with someone at one of the local bicycle specialty shops who is going to spend a couple hours advising me on how to pick up a good used bike. I've learned about upcoming road races that sound like a lot of fun, and one person has even invited me to be join his team on an upcoming race. All this happened in two weeks, and it started with me talking to one friend about my desire to start cycling. People don't just ask you to join a team, and complete strangers don't just agree to take time out of their schedules to give free advice. These folks are attracted to helping me for the same reason I was attracted to seeking them out: we share a common passion and that shared experience is one of the most compelling forces in life. A great pageant of opportunity surrounds us. Passion is your ticket to the show.

Balance is Passion, Passion is Balance

One of the things that makes work-life balancing difficult is the implied separation between the work and life. Work is work, not life. Life is life, not work. We spend our time struggling with what we feel we must do at work so we can have the life we want. Work impinges on life; we work way too much (especially here in the U.S.) and lament the life we are missing out on while we are at the office. Life impinges on work; we feel we are passed up for career opportunities because we can't put in the late hours anymore and still be with our kids. Some of us, notably working moms, go so far as to quit work because of this tension. It's as though we've decided work and life are two opposite and incompatible forces, one necessary the other desired, both competing for the same piece of our soul. The only way to have one is at the expense of the other, and balancing is the act of deciding which career aspirations you are willing to abandon, and which life experiences you are willing to miss.

One of the things that passion has done for me is to help me erase this destructive distinction between work and life. I don't see myself as two warring personalities any more; rather, I am one person pursing a host of passions that I find most compelling for me. From when I get up to when I turn in, I am all about having fun doing the things that turn me on. There is no "Career Paul" separate from "Father Paul" or "Husband Paul," and I do not view my life as a series of decisions where I can only engage in one thing (say being with my kids) at the expense of another (say going out with my wife). Instead, I see each day as a series of opportunities to advance *all* the causes I've got going at any given moment.

A good day is one where I meet my commitments and accomplish as much as I can in as many aspects of my life as is possible. If that means doing "opposing" things together, then fine. If that means being unorthodox, I don't really care. For instance, several years ago when I was opening my own business, I needed to look for office space. My first daughter was an infant at the time and I loved going out with her strapped into one of those "front loaded" rigs that holds babies across your chest facing outward so they can look around. I spent several happy days meeting real estate reps with my daughter strapped to my chest. Nobody complained (in fact, I think they found it refreshing), my daughter and I had a great time, and I found a good deal on office space about a block away from a great running trail where I knew I'd be able to go for a run on my lunch hour. That's work, kids, and exercise all rolled into one.

As you begin to master work-life balancing you will know you are on the right track when the artificial distinction between work and life disappears and in its place emerges a desire to focus on whatever is important to you regardless of the label our culture puts on it. It's not about being superman or wonder woman and it's not about trying to be all things to all people. It's about being the important things to yourself. There is no distinction between work and life, only a pursuit of what matters to you. Activities flow into one another because you are always doing the same thing—pursuing passion—instead of trying to separate your life into arbitrary compartments.

Passion reduces the amount of energy we typically waste in life, making us more productive by freeing up hours wasted trying to guess what we "should" do. It gives us an instant decision mechanism because we know the right thing when we see it. And it relieves us of doubt. We end up producing more because we are excited about what we are doing, which people can't help but notice and which, in turn, opens doors to more opportunities. Best of all, passion simplifies life by erasing the difference between work and life. When you tap into your passion, it makes everything easier. Like Tennyson's Sir Galahad, you will find your strength "…is as the strength of ten because [your] heart is pure." Or perhaps even better, like the Grinch, you will find you will have "the strength of ten grinches—plus two!"

Story: A Tale of Two Employees

Imagine you are a manager. You are faced with a decision to promote someone in your department. It's one of those great things you get to do as a manager, to reward someone for all the hard work they have put in to the job. Typically there are multiple people on your team whom you could promote. The hard part is choosing one over another.

When you make such a decision, several things go on in your mind. Who deserves it the most? Who would be best for the business? Who is dependable? Who is the best self-starter? And not least of all, with whom do you like to work the most? After all, when you promote this person you are bringing them closer to you, moving them into a position where they will be working with you more than they have in the past. If you don't get along it's going to be difficult. They might even take your job one day. That kind of opportunity is not something you would bestow upon someone you don't like.

Now, let's make the story more interesting. Imagine you have boiled it down to two people you could promote. One is your "standard" kind of employee. He comes to work at the right time, and stays the right number of hours.

He is driven and does all the right things. He tries to know the right people, say the right things, and participate at all the right functions and activities. In short, he's capable but he's a "brown noser," someone who wants to climb the corporate ladder and is doing all the things that he believes he's supposed to do to make that happen. In fact, just for fun, let's call him Mr. Brown.

Your second choice is Ms. Gusto. She has a completely different approach. She comes to work wearing her passions on her sleeve. She is enthusiastic about what she is doing, perhaps even getting ahead of the team at times. Because she is so "in to" what she's doing, she often thinks ahead and spontaneously brings new opportunities to your attention that she thinks will help the team. She doesn't seem to think overtly about career path; in fact, when you talk to her about career it is almost as if it is an afterthought for her, something she has to squeeze in among all the other interesting stuff she is doing in her job. She doesn't try to go to the right functions, she seeks out the ones where she feels she can have fun and be a useful participant and then jumps in and takes an active role. She will promote herself, but she is also happy to promote other team members as well, especially if it gives her a chance to spread her enthusiasm. In short, she's not trying to do the right thing for her career, she's simply trying to do the right thing.

Now I ask you: whom are you going to promote? Whom do you think the team respects more? Who is more reliable? Who is more of a self-starter? Which of these two candidates is better for the business? In my book it's a slam dunk in favor of Ms. Gusto. Her enthusiasm is contagious and inspirational, and the new manager will need to be able to inspire the team to follow him or her. That doesn't happen for someone who is primarily focused on themselves. The new manager will need a vision for the part of the business he or she will be running that goes beyond their self interest. Will Ms. Gusto sometimes go too far or too fast? Probably. But people are much more patient with over enthusiasm than they are with naked ambition. I'd much rather manage someone I know is avidly promoting the business versus merely promoting themselves.

Now turn the story around and ask yourself whom you would rather be. If promotion is what you are after, clearly Ms. Gusto's route has the greater opportunity. Ironic, isn't it, that by not trying so hard for a promotion, Ms. Gusto maximizes her chances of getting just that opportunity?

Story: Always On—Curse or Opportunity?

I had an interesting experience this past year in a panel discussion about modern work styles. The subject was the "virtual workforce" which is a fancy term for saying that nowadays with all the electronic gizmos we've invented, it's possible for you to literally be working all the time. Thanks to wireless technology, laptops, and blackberries you too can answer email while in bed. Who needs sleep? After all, we're Americans and we're not about to let anyone get a step on us. If that means answering email while we are in the shower, then so be it. If we remain #1 in anything, it will be in numbers of heart attacks before the age of 40.

I'm teasing, of course, but it was with a smug sense of knowing the other panel members would surely present a negative view of the ubiquity of communications that I approached my participation in this panel discussion. I expected the members to join in on a general trashing of virtualization. Our goal for the discussion was to lend our insights about technology and work, making predictions about the use of technology in the next decade. "Would there be a backlash?" the moderator asked us. "What trends should employers expect to see in their workforce and how could they position themselves with an environment that would attract potential employees?" This is no small issue for companies as they look to a future of more competition for a shrinking pool of employees, which is exactly where we are headed with the baby-boom generation about to hit retirement.

As I expected, a majority of panel members did, in fact, agree with the backlash theory. However, that view was not universal. Most surprising was the fact that some panel members were almost confused by the question. That's not exactly accurate; it wasn't as though they didn't understand the issue, so much as they expressed difficulty in understanding why technology should automatically be considered a negative. Amazingly, they were not the youngest members of the panel. These were 50- and 60- somethings who grew up without the benefit of any of the neat toys we have today. For them, a radio that played crackly rock and roll would have been cutting edge, and it would have been the size of a paperback book.

Naturally, they piqued my interest immediately. Out of the whole panel these were the folks I would have pegged as the most vocal anti-technologists. What bound them together? One was from the U.S., another from India. They had different backgrounds, different career paths, and were even of different religions. What was it about their attitude that allowed them to welcome technologies that everyone else in the room saw as an intrusion?

It turned out the answer was that they both had something missing in common. If that sounds a little weird, it was a little weird: they both had not endorsed a cultural belief that bound the rest of us together and held us back. I finally understood when the U.S. gentleman expressed a typical "day in his life" of using technology. "You probably would not be able to guess," he explained, "what it is I am doing at any point in the day. I might be logged in to the Internet to answer emails from work, or I might be sending an instant message to my daughter at college. I might be on a conference call or I might be planning a dinner out with my wife. Work-life balance doesn't have any meaning for me; at any point in time I might be doing either one. If I want a break, I take a break. If the phone rings, I might not answer it. All these devices do have 'off' buttons, you know."

I wanted to stand up and applaud. What a great attitude. No separation between work and life. No feelings of compulsion. He had not bought in to this ridiculous, yet deeply entrenched, attitude that work and life are in-compatible. And yet, this gentleman was obviously someone who would be labeled "successful." He had been invited to participate on this world wide panel. His travel costs and time were paid for; obviously he is highly regarded. I don't know if he has always had this point of view or if it's something he has developed over time. Either way he is a great example of the power of letting yourself be guided by *interests*, instead of *stereotypes*. There is no demarcation between his work and his life, as he said. His passions are his guide. The world of technology, which is so confusing for so many of us, is just another tool to him to enable the kind of life he wants. And at any point in time, that's exactly what you will see him doing: living the life he wants.

Story: Mom's Week Off

Speaking of blurring the distinction between work and life, how many of you have ever considered using telecommuting to improve the life of someone else? Typically, if you have telecommuting options they enable you to improve your own lifestyle. But they can also be a wonderful way to improve the lifestyle of your spouse, or at least give her a gift every husband should give every wife: Mom's week off.

It's no surprise that IBM has been consistently voted one of the best employers for several years running now. IBM has invested heavily in telecommuting as an option for its employees. The virtualized workplace is something IBM not only talks about and sells, but lives as well. And it's not just something that makes employees happy; when you have over 300,000 employees and you can encourage almost a quarter of them to do their job without an office, that is a huge savings in rent, electricity, air conditioning, heating, you name it. That's a great benefit, but it can also come in handy when you want to do something extra special for your wife.

I was at a company gathering one day and got talking to a guy who does project management for IBM. It turns out he's traveled all over the world to manage projects, but not in the way you might first think. We got talking about how great it was to be able to telecommute to work and he told me he has worked all over the world, but not because his job took him there. Instead, he and his family take long summer "vacations." For instance, last year they decided they would all like to learn more about their heritage (he is of Italian descent) and spend 6 weeks in Italy. So they all took an intense course in Italian and spent a big chunk of the summer on the Amalfi coast. Sweet. How did he get so much time off? He didn't. Where was the team he was managing? Mostly in the U.S. Now *that's* telecommuting.

It got me thinking. My wife, the best lady in the world, had been working non-stop for the last six years (since our first was born). What better gift than some time off? And not just Mom's night off—how about Mom's *week* off? Why not? I was working at a company that allowed me to telecommute. True, for most folks that means they can stay in their jammies all day if they like, but the Internet runs just as fast at my Mom's house as it does at my house. That's the thing about telecommuting; it's not location-specific. Plus, most of my team was spread out across the U.S. anyway. It wasn't like we had weekly face-to-face meetings. I could spend the day sipping joe at the local coffee shop and my team wouldn't be affected in the least.

So that's what we did. I took my kids and spent two weeks with my Mom. My siblings have stayed close to home (I was the only acorn that fell far from the oak) so it was great for my kids. It gave them a chance to be with their grandmother and play with their cousins on a regular basis over an extended period. To make up for the extra help I knew I'd need during the day, I scheduled, in advance, which days my kids would be with their cousins and which days I'd need to line up a baby sitter. My Mom knew a local high school girl who was interested in picking up some extra cash, and a couple of phone calls later I had my temp-nanny lined up. We weren't sure how much we would all miss my wife, though, so we decided to make the two weeks half work, half vacation and my wife joined us for the second week. But that first week was all hers. All the peace and quite she wanted, or the option to stay late at work too. No debate over whether it was going to be a chick flick we rented or the latest action movie. Nobody she had to answer to except herself.

I love that story because it is so obvious once you think of it, and yet it took us six years to figure it out! The opportunity was right there in front of my face, and I couldn't see it because I had placed the concept of telecommuting squarely in the "work" box which was distinct from the "life" box. Once I saw the silliness of the distinction, it opened up a whole new way of living and working.

Story: Less Time, More Results

Here is one of my favorite stories about the power of passion and how it really can give you "the strength of ten." It gets me close to that danger zone of feeling like I am bragging again, so you will have to forgive me if it comes across sounding smug. But it is the best story I can think of to illustrate how you can literally get more done in less time, and if I have to have you think of me as a show-off to get the point across, then so be it.

It has to do with how I finished my Ph.D. in Computer Science and literally got more done in less time. The odd thing is that I *wasn't trying* to do more than anyone else. It was one of those happy accidents that occasionally arise in life, and it only occurred to me years later why I was able to get so much done in such a short space of time. As you read the story now, it may sound like I knew what I was doing. I didn't. In fact, I can guarantee you that I was not the top in my class, and I know for a fact that my entrance exam marks put me in about the middle of the pack—certainly not any kind of genius. But to me that makes the story even more compelling because it means you don't have to be "special" or have anything remotely like a "master plan" to reap the benefits of a passion-focused life. You just have to follow your heart, which is what we all secretly want to do anyway.

To complete a masters and doctorate degree program in the sciences typically takes six or seven years. When I signed on for my tour of duty, the average time to get a Ph.D. in Computer Science was six and a half years. Yet, I managed to complete both degrees in a combined four years, over two years ahead of schedule. And to make it even more incredible, I did it without working on any weekends (except, of course, studying before exams) plus I golfed twice a week. So it wasn't as if I was spending all my time working; I had a lot of fun. Sounds unbelievable, doesn't it? Surely I am lying or there is a catch somewhere. I promise you there isn't. The only thing I did differently from everyone else was to stay focused on the area of research that had so captured my interest. My secret: I followed my passion.

There is a reason why graduate school, especially in the sciences, typically takes a long time. Doctorate work is unlike other kinds of schooling because there is no structure to guaranty when you will finish your work. True, you do have course work, and that does take place in scheduled chunks of time, but the bulk of your work must be original and you must, at some point, have done enough significant work that a body of your peers determines you are worthy of receiving your doctorate degree. Compare this to, say, getting your M.D. or a degree in law. In those fields, a course of study and exams with a set schedule must be completed and, once completed, you then pass a "bar" or a "board" test and you are done.

Not so with a Ph.D. You do have qualifying exams to take, but these only qualify you to become a candidate for your Ph.D. Once a candidate, you must come up with an original idea and plot your own course for proving the validity of your approach. I understand now why this open sort of structure is one of the main reasons people take so long to get their degrees. You are largely on your own, and it is easy to let yourself wander. It's easy, for example, to feel lost or to feel like what you are doing is insignificant. It is also easy to feel like whatever you may have discovered has surely been thought of by someone else before you. In short, it's easy to doubt what you are doing, and that leads to hand wringing and slower decision making. To phrase it with the language used earlier in this chapter, there is a huge potential to add friction to your life. You are largely on your own, without a set structure, so it's easy to *doubt* yourself, which *slows down your decisions* and generally *adds overhead* to everything you do. In short, graduate school presents an abundance of opportunities to get bogged down.

What made the experience different for me was simply that I had an interest to pursue. I was so interested in my topic of study, which I had hit upon before even applying to graduate school, that I accidentally avoided most of the overhead. I was focused, so it was easier for me to see the path that led most directly to what I wanted to study. While many of my classmates spent the first couple of years trying to find a topic they liked and a professor to advise them, I spent that time with my advisor working on my research. I had selected my school, in fact, because that was where my advisor was a professor. I had met him before I even applied, and had made a point to talk with him and sound him out with my ideas, outlining the main thrust of my interest. Keep in mind that advisors don't advise one student at a time. They work with multiple students on many different projects. They can't keep up with all the details, so they look for a good general idea and depend upon their students to take the initiative. Again, my passion gave me an advantage. I didn't have to figure everything out in advance; I could just follow my instincts. I also had one final advantage. I didn't spend a lot of time worrying about what I would do after I graduated. I was too busy having fun pursuing my topic of study. That meant I didn't get into the debates some of my classmates did about whether this advisor or that one would be more likely to help with a career, or which journal or conference was the best one for publications. I just did my thing. And because I liked it so much, it was easy to do and to do well.

How did this matter? Well, if you could have logged the time that my classmates and I spent doing work versus worrying about doing work, you would have seen a big difference in our schedules. I spent almost no time "off topic." Imagine being able to reclaim a few hours of every day over a four year period. At two hours a day, five days a week, that's over 500 hours a year. For a regular 40-hour week, that's 25% overhead. If you add it up over four years, it amounts to almost *an entire extra year* of time. So you see, I wasn't smarter or better than anyone else. I just ran my engine more efficiently.

What if I had made a mistake? What if I had picked a topic that turned out to be a dud? I might not have finished in four years, but I would *still* have been more efficient. I could have wasted an entire year's worth of effort and still been at the same level as my peers! More likely I would have found out in less than a year that my first topic was a dud, and either turned my attention to a new topic or else I might have simply dropped out and gone on to the next most interesting thing. Either way, I would still be operating at a 25% advantage over the typical process that included a lot of extra overhead for worry.

There is a temptation to take this kind of story and turn it into a competition, as in "here's the secret of how you can outdo your peers." I think that would be a mistake, and would obscure the larger point. That kind of hyper competitive thinking gets you into the whole negative side of grades and keeping up and all that crap.[10] The real moral of the story is to compare the two different ways my *own* experience with graduate school could have been. On the one hand, I could have spent a lot more time worrying, and taken a lot longer to accomplish the research I knew I wanted to do in the first place. I could have taken six or seven years to finish something that really only needed four years of my time. And I could have had a lot less fun, because the time I would have wasted on worry could not have been spent golfing or goofing off. Instead, I gave in to what I wanted to do. I spent most of my time actually doing what I really liked, and as a result I finished sooner

---

[10] Or perhaps it's just that being the type-A that I am, feeling competitive is never a problem—I usually have the opposite problem of trying to keep my competitive feelings in check.

and got back into the workforce making a real salary sooner. And I had a blast along the way.

As I said earlier, it turned out that I fell into this mode of working by accident. I just "did it" without really knowing any of the stuff I've written about in this book. But the results are just as compelling as if I'd planned it all out. Following your passion allows you to spend your life doing what you want to do, and it frees up an amazing amount of time for all those other things we call "balance" that make it all worth while.

Story: The Opportunity Escalator

Before we leave this chapter on passion, I owe you one more story. I talked about how passion leads to compounding opportunities, and I will relate specifically how that has happened to me. Once again, I will have to apologize for getting on the brag wagon, but it's the best story I have. Maybe some of you who read my book will send in your own stories and I can use them instead in the next edition.

I've made the claim that when you follow your passion, opportunity leads to more opportunity. I've called it the "compounding interest of opportunity" and said that the reason some people seem to have "all the luck" has nothing at all to do with luck or planning or the right connections, but instead has everything to do with being connected to their passion. Here is a story about exactly how that happened to me. It's a story without an end because I am still reaping the benefits of the "luck" that seems to be following me around, all because I am doing what I enjoy.

At the time this story begins I had been working at IBM for two years. At a company the size of IBM, two years is not very much time to get connected. It's just not physically possible. Think about it: there are over 300,000 employees at IBM. If only 10% of them are the "right" people to know, and if I could somehow magically know which people were on that special list, I would still have to meet more than 41 new people *every day* to meet them all in just two years. So there is no way I could claim to be in a position of having any kind of extensive network within the company. And yet, I ended up working on one of the CEO's pet projects. You would think some kind of giant magical hand had plucked me out of the sea of employees to give me such an assignment. The reality was that it all came about because of one comment I made by email. That single, small initiative on my part was like a stone that started an avalanche.

Here's what happened. I was working for a group inside of IBM called Extreme Blue.[11] Extreme Blue focuses on bringing in new talent into IBM through a summer intern experience focused on innovation. The interns are given a business problem and asked to build a new product or service around it. At the end of each summer, Extreme Blue gathers the members of all projects together to present their project results at an "Expo" which essentially amounts to a science fair for grown ups. It is held near IBM's corporate headquarters.

During one particular summer while I was working with Extreme Blue, we were lucky enough to have our CEO

---

[11] I know I've given the background on Extreme Blue before, but I never know what order people are going to read the book and I want each of the stories to hang together. Sorry for any boring repetition.

show up at our Expo. As you can imagine, he is incredibly busy and has huge demands upon his time, but he graciously stopped by to give a lift to the students, putting what I am sure for many of them was the icing on the cake of a fantastic summer experience. I know he enjoyed it as well; he said in his remarks that visiting with a bunch of young, energetic, people compared quite favorably to enduring the slings and arrows of Wall Street. He left us all feeling incredibly pumped up. It deserved a good "thank you" on our part.

So a few days after his visit I sat down to write him a "thank you" email. I knew it needed to be short, and I guessed it probably might not even be read. I mean c'mon; they guy is running a multi-billion dollar corporation with a whole lot on his plate. My little thank you email is just not going to be that high on the priority list. So I had no illusions, but grace dictated that I send him a note.

Now, here is where the opportunity comes in. Watch what happened.

Every day, IBM publishes stories on its internal web site about items of general interest to all employees. It just so happened that when I was getting ready to compose my thank you email, the story of the day was about how our CEO was leading (co-chairing, actually) a national effort to study how the U.S. could remain competitive as an innovator in light of changes overseas. It was called the National Innovation Initiative (NII) and it was to be run by a Washington group called the Council on Competitiveness.[12] Other countries had figured out our formula for success, or so it seemed, and the obvious question loomed

---

[12] You can see details at www.compete.org

before us: what can the U.S. do to bolster its innovation culture so as to keep pace with the changing world? After all, countries like India and China have much larger populations that we do, and there is nothing stopping them from creating an educational system that can produce many, many more scientists, engineers and technologists than we can produce in the U.S. If the engine of innovation runs on such skills, what can the U.S. possibly do to keep up?

I won't get into the details of what the U.S. can do except to say that I am very bullish on the possibilities.[13] The point for this story is that I saw the report on the launch of the NII effort and it spoke to me. Innovation is one of my passions. It was why I got up in the morning to go to work. And there I had a story before me about how my own CEO was doing something to try to make a difference. It was very inspiring. So when I wrote to thank our CEO for his appearance at Extreme Blue's Expo, I also told him that I thought his work on the NII was inspiring. I added that I was interested in participating if that was appropriate, and if it was not, that I would be cheering for him either way.

Now, some would say that was a crazy thing to do. Write to the CEO? And just ask? Good grief, man, you're going to look like a complete idiot. Sure, that was a possibility; after all, I had no particular reason to think I had any more to add than anyone else, and I would typically not even consider writing to the CEO without a very good reason to do so. After all, it never helps anyone to send a useless email—that would just waste my time and

---

[13] You can see a full report on the positive actions the U.S. can take a www.compete.org (look for the "Innovate America" report).

his time. But I had a reason to write him a thank you (opportunity), and given this NII effort was something I was truly passionate about (another opportunity), it seemed worth mentioning my enthusiasm and willingness to volunteer my free time. I was willing to *embrace the opportunity*, so long as it was a match for the goals of others. If not, there was no loss to me, and no shame in volunteering my time to help out.

Within two days I got a reply. "Let's get Paul involved" was what it said.

And so it started. My first reaction was to write to my boss and say "Holy cow! I think I just scared the crap out of myself!" I really had not anticipated I would have much of an opportunity to be involved, so it caught me off guard. But it was exciting too. This was the kind of stuff I lived and breathed, so to be involved at all was an honor. I eagerly went to a meeting for the launch of the NII study, yet fully expecting my role would be something very junior. That was OK; I was there simply to help out. In fact, I recall even telling myself (as an aid to help me get over feeling quite nervous) that "all I had to do was look for the *opportunities* to help out." "You don't have to have an opinion about everything," I told myself, "just be yourself and the opportunities where you can make a difference will present themselves."

I was assigned to work on a subgroup of the NII inside of IBM that was focused on skills. That made sense; I was working as a recruiter in a program that was all about how to find the most talented interns and give them the best innovation skills and training. Our skills group was a team of 10 people, from across a spectrum of perspectives at IBM. All of them were senior people. That presented another opportunity. Somebody had to help coordinate the group's efforts. Somebody had to step up to make sure that 10 very busy people could be kept informed. Somebody had to collect their thoughts and ideas, and make sure they were written up, so the group's results could be combined with the thoughts of about 400 other individuals across the country who were going to be contributing to the process. Somebody had to take more time out of their busy schedule to do all this coordination. Like Ms. Gusto, I was eager. It must have stood out. I was asked to coordinate the group's efforts. I accepted.

From there things led to a series of meetings where I tried to make sure everyone's opinions could be collected. Much of the work was coordination; as you can imagine, keeping hundreds of people across many different organizations all going in the same direction is hard. Part of this coordination involved national meetings, parallel to the meetings we were having inside of IBM. Here, another opportunity presented itself when a calendar conflict meant someone from IBM needed to volunteer to attend a national meeting in Washington to coordinate the efforts of all the sub-teams across the country working on the skills issue. Once again, I was asked. Once again, I accepted.

The national group turned out to be much like the internal group: lots of busy people all with great points of view and all with calendars filled to the brim. Again I accepted the role of collecting inputs from across the national group members and took on the task of writing up a white paper that other members of the national group could then tweak by editing their own sections. This time my effort was particularly useful as it helped the national skills group out of a last minute calendar bind. We produced what I think was a great combined effort with key inputs from across a good cross-section of perspectives.

The head of the national skills group, from MIT, thanked me for my effort. IBM appreciated my efforts too and gave me a special award.

All of this came from one opportunity. I let my passion and enthusiasm guide me, and each time it led to more opportunities. From the outside, it must have seemed like I had "all the luck." From my own perspective, I was mostly just having fun, doing something I cared about, trying to help where I thought it was needed most. I definitely did not plan any of this, but I don't think it was all one big accident either. It's a perfect illustration of the kinds of things that happen when you focus on your passion and respond to the matching opportunities. It's a story of how that simple approach leads to opportunities that feed on themselves, because passion is contagious. It's like creating your own virus to drive your life forward. Opportunities are out there, all around us. If we look through the lens of our passion they are easy to spot, and once we "catch the bug" our own enthusiasm will generate more opportunities.

But How Do I Find My Passion?

One of the most common questions I get when I talk about passion goes something like this, "Fine, Paul, I get what you are saying, but none of this makes any difference if I don't know what my passion is. How do I figure out what my passion is in the first place?"

I'm going to punt on that question for now because I will have more to say about it in the next chapter. I'll give you a hint, though: passion is *not* something you *figure out*, it's something you *admit*. And you will hear it calling out to you loud and clear only when you are quiet.

105

4 Reinforce With Rituals

Principle 4: Make the time to build <u>regular</u> reinforcement rituals into your schedule. You will need these to keep your balance. Very few of us pay attention to regular maintenance activities because their repetitive nature can lull us into thinking they amount to wasted time. They do not. They may not be glamorous, but they are essential—you will fail without them.

Running With the Herd Without Getting Stampeded

The System. The "them," the "they," the great unseen I-know-they-are-looking-over-my-shoulder kind of feeling we all carry around with us. You know what I'm talking about. We call it peer pressure, and it's a living force, crashing around like a blind rhinoceros, completely unpredictable, never intentionally malicious, yet brutal to anything caught in its path. Who knew that people would literally fight over cabbage patch dolls at the Toys-R-Us? Does that seem ludicrous now or what? 'Course we're past all that kind of thing today, right? Ha! Here's another one for you. The other day I opened a Wall Street Journal and read an article about how women are now lining up to spend upwards of $1,200 for a pair of sandals. *Sandals.* A few years ago, sandals were things you bought at Wall-Mart for $12. That's about as smart as us men shelling out top dollar for the latest cool gizmo that we "just gotta have" and then leaving it to collect dust (yeah me too, I have a closet full of them).

Fashion is only the most obvious of what one might call the "pendulum phenomenon." This is The System's ability to arbitrarily generate what feels like a mass judgment against you. The System has its swings, what is popular changes, and you can suddenly find yourself unexpectedly sticking out like a sore thumb. Take politics, for instance. Let's say you are a fiscal conservative. You don't think the government should spend more than it takes in. In the Carter years, that would have earned you a "conservative" label. In the Clinton years of balanced budgets, you would have fit in well with the "liberals." And now here you are, wearing sandals that don't have a designer label on them because when you bought them there *were* no sandals with designer labels on them and you still think the government shouldn't deficit-spend. Good grief! You need to get with the program! Quick—take out a home equity loan right away so you can afford to buy a couple of pairs of the right kind of sandals, and then you too can be safely plunging headlong into more debt just like your government. Heaven forbid you swing against the pendulum!

I'm being outrageous, of course, but you get my point— or do you? Perhaps not, because I am making a point that may be rather more subtle than you might realize.

Why Balance Can Feel Wrong

What I am saying is that if you want to live a balanced life, then *you will feel like you stick out*. Expect it. It is unavoidable. Human beings don't live balanced lives as a general rule, so if you want to live a balanced life, then you should expect to stand out. We live in herds, and the herd instinct is incredibly strong. You are supposed to go where the herd goes, and if the herd decides to jump off a cliff then you are supposed to jump right along with everyone else. Sound far fetched? What if the herd thinks you need to spend 60 hours a week at work to be a success? What if the herd thinks you can't be a working mom and still be doing justice to your children? What if the herd thinks that once you have children you have to drive a mini-van or an SUV? What if the herd thinks you have to answer email on the weekends? What if the herd says the only way to be an attractive woman is if you have a D cup? What if the herd says the only way to be an attractive man is to be tall, have a full head of hair, and make lots of money? How far fetched does it sound now?

Folks, the point is that The System is *arbitrary*. That's so important I'll say it again: The System is *arbitrary*. You can pick on our culture if you like and try to lay the blame on that,[14] but the truth is that *any* human group is going to swing to extremes, for no particular reason, and those extremes will be labeled "normal." I'm no sociologist so I can't tell you the theory behind why this is so, but my guess is it has something to do with the fact that we're such puny creatures compared to things like lions and tigers and bears that we learned a long time ago the only way to survive was in a group. Safety lies in numbers, as the saying goes. Consequently, we can't help but want to be part of the herd, so when the herd moves we feel an intense pull to go with the crowd. And of course, wherever the crowd goes is the "right" direction, because…well… because that's where the crowd is going and, by circular

---

[14] Of course, we know that blame gets you nowhere—see Chapter 2.

reasoning, that must be right for the crowd because the crowd says it's right.

For whatever weird reason, these shifts in herd direction are arbitrary. In particular, they are *not rational* decisions. How can it be rational to spend $1,200 on a pair of sandals? How can it be rational to think the only way to be a success is if you spend so much time at work that you never get to see your kids? That's not rational. It may or may not be wrong, but it is certainly not rational. It is *arbitrary*, and that is the key. The herd is not governed by rationality but instead by whatever happens to look good to the herd at the time. It's more accidental than purposeful. It's *arbitrary*.

The problem from a balance perspective is that being in balance is all about *not* being arbitrary. Living a balanced life means *purposefully* embracing the things that are important to you, and arranging your life to suit. It is not about doing whatever the herd thinks, whenever the herd thinks it. It's all about doing what *you* think, to address *your* needs, so that *you* can be happy. Who knows, maybe you like being single, you don't ever want to have kids, and working 60 hours a week for you is pure joy. If so, your biggest challenge may end up being defending your choices against all your friends who have read this book and decided to spend less time at work. The point is this: balance means taking the time to tap in to what really matters to *you*, not what you were told *should* matter to you. All of which means that you must expect you will be forced to think differently from the herd from time to time. The herd mentality will not always work for you, and in such cases you will have to do your own thinking. It will be different. Your decisions will "stick out." As a result, you will feel awkward.

That is why balance will sometimes feel wrong.

It's also why I can guarantee you that you will fall off the wagon. You will backslide. You will sincerely and honestly mean to live a balanced life, and yet you will find yourself stumbling into herd behavior that you really don't like because nobody can resist the herd instinct forever. Nobody is that aloof.

So what can you do about it? Are you doomed to eventual imbalance? No, there are specific actions you can take to get yourself back on track and to minimize the time spent out of balance. And by happy coincidence, I have some ideas on just that point that I would like to share with you.

How to Get Back On Track

We all suffer setbacks as we try to pursue the goals we set for ourselves. That's no mystery to anyone. Just take a look at all the people who make New Year's resolutions to live a healthier lifestyle. In January and February, the crowds are so thick at the gym that you can't buy time on that stair-master machine which will be begging for use come April or May. People get busy, things come up, and we find we somehow can't remember where we last left that good intention which seemed so unshakably important at holiday time.

What's fascinating to me is that we don't get up, dust ourselves off, and get back at it. Why, for example, don't we see a resurgence of participation at the gym in the summer? Why do people seem to just give up? For that matter, what's *really* odd is that people don't give up entirely, because you will see them back at it almost exactly one year later. What the heck is *that* all about?

111

What, may I ask, is so special about the dead of winter that causes this momentary blip in determination?

To me this is all incredibly interesting because it says there is a regular patter, a *ritual* if you will, that we seem to be following. And it's a powerful thing this ritual. A whole industry is built around it for selling us expensive home exercise equipment that we use for three months then forget about as it gathers dust in the basement or a spare bedroom. The ritual is there, it's repeatable, and you can take it to the bank (literally). But the most compelling thing about this ritual to me is that it is positive at its core; it forgives us for our mistakes and pushes us back in the right direction.

Imagine what would happen if you could tap in to this ritualistic part of your psyche and turn it to your advantage. What if you built your own rituals, and made them dance to the rhythm you set for them? What if you *deliberately created rituals* to renew your commitment to the important things in your life? Do you think that balance would be any easier to obtain? You bet it would. In fact, I would claim it is exactly these kinds of rituals of renewal that are essential to maintaining a balanced life. Let me tell you about a few rituals that I think are critical, and follow up with some specific stories of how I build them into my routine.

Ritual 1: Get Quiet, Hear Your Passion

At the end of the last chapter, I promised that would talk more about how to find your passion. I also hinted at the fact that passion is not something you have to figure out. It is something you already know. It's not in a book, and it's not "out there" waiting for you to find it. It's personal, it comes from within; otherwise it wouldn't be passion because it wouldn't be genuinely part of you. The trick is to give yourself a way to admit to yourself what you are passionate about. And that is where the "quiet ritual" comes in.

You probably already know plenty of "quiet" techniques if you stop to think about it. Holy men, for instance, who go into the wilderness alone and fast until they are visited by a dream or a vision that reveals to them the focus of their ministry. Bill Gates' twice-a-year "think week" ritual of spending five days alone to reset his perspective. Christ's wandering in the desert for 40 days and 40 nights. The CEO of the Japanese company (I think it was Sony) whose habits included spending quiet time every morning in his garden. Teddy Roosevelt, undeniably one of America's most passionate presidents, who used to leave Washington for months at a time, heading out to the Dakota territories to be by himself. What gives? Why all the quiet time? What is the connection between being still and being passionate and why does it work?

It all has to do with the *opposite* of quiet—noise—and with our good old friend the herd. Think about it. What if your passion is for something that isn't what your parents always wanted for you? What if you were supposed to grow up to be a doctor but you hate the site of blood? What if you grew up in the city and all you want to do is hang out in the country and raise horses? What if you really want to be an engineer but you come from a family that doesn't value education and expects you to get an honest job doing something like lawn maintenance just like the rest of the men in your family?[15] It's impossible to grow up without feeling the need to belong to a group, therefore the influence of others on us is strong. Even if your parents, your friends, and everyone else around you is perfectly happy and balanced, they will have their own passions that will not necessarily match yours. Every one of us is different and has a different inner muse, which makes it inevitable that you will find yourself being different and, therefore, suffering the judgment of the herd.

This is where noise comes in. If you don't want to face the fear of sticking out, then having a lot of noise is really convenient. You can simply avoid your passions by burying them in noise. And when it comes to noise, life in America in the 21st century offers us the ultimate in convenience, providing us with a cornucopia of easy ways to keep our schedules overflowing. You've got that email that has to be answered, or the five different after school activities for each of your 2.3 children that you have to fit into your schedule, or the blackberry you carry with you everywhere, or that cell phone or PDA that you need to constantly check to make sure you stay in the know. And if that's not enough for you, there is all the maintenance work for keeping up appearances to fill in your spare time, like shopping to make sure you have the right clothes, or spending time at the gym, or cutting the grass, trimming the bushes, painting the barn…the list is endless. If you want, you can find a way to create enough noise that you can hide from your passion forever. You never have to be afraid of sticking out—you can just stay too busy for that.

---

[15] I know I like to exaggerate, but I'm not making this one up—I actually interviewed a young man once from the inner city of Houston who was applying to college and was in precisely this situation.

Which is what makes quiet time the most powerful ally you can have. It is the first, best, and most important renewal ritual you can build in to your life. And let me nip something in the bud here right away. I am *not* talking about rest. I am *not* talking about taking a break. Those things are also critically important, but they are not what I mean by "quiet time." I'm talking about contemplation, not vacation. I mean time to sit, alone, when you are well rested, and just think. No particular agenda, no particular problems to solve—just time to sit and think about you, what you want out of life, and to do it in a setting where you don't feel pushed, rushed, harassed, harried, or under the gun in any way.

Remove the noise and you will tap in to what you really want. You will hear the inner tune that is uniquely your own. My own method is to give myself an hour every morning when I first get up and my mind is the most rested. If I wait until after I get to work, or if I try to wait to the end of the day, I tend to get so busy or work myself to such exhaustion that any attempt at quiet time really becomes recovery time. It's also important to make this a regular ritual so that the voice of passion inside you has a chance to be heard. For me, it's about an hour a day, every day. Most of us don't have the luxury of being able to take 40 days and 40 nights off, so we need another way to get consistent quiet time. A daily ritual of quiet time—time when you are well rested—is the most important ritual you can have for a balanced life.

When you get quiet, don't put any particular pressure on yourself. In fact, the fewer expectations you can put on yourself the better. Just take the time to be still and to reflect on yourself. Put all worries out of your mind; you'll have the rest of the day for those. After all, we are only talking about an hour here, so no matter how urgent something may feel, just forget about it for an hour. Imagine all your problems are solved, you have all the money you need, you have all the expectations met, and nobody is hounding you. Pretend that everything you "have to do" is done, and now you are living a life of leisure. Given that state of mind ask yourself "what would I be doing? What would I do for free, just because I love to do it?"

I guarantee you that when you do this, what you really want to do will pop into your head. I've done this little exercise countless times with people that I mentor (and for myself) and the result is always the same. I say "what do you really want to do with your life? What really turns you on?" Their first reaction is to say "well I don't know—I just have so many 'chores' I have to do, like A and B and C…" I respond with "OK, imagine I've waved a magic wand and made all those worries go away. What would you do?" That's when they will say "Oh, well, if we're pretending, then I'd say I've always wanted to do such-and-such, but I can't because <insert-your-favorite-excuse-here>." Did you hear it? The passion pops right out, followed by all the rubbish they have used for years to bury their desires (for those keeping track this will sound a lot like the blame game in Chapter 2). When you get quiet, and you take away the worries, the passion is right there, just under the surface, probably hiding under a layer of blame to keep it safely locked away.

Do this every day for a month and you will know what you want to do. Do it every day for a prolonged period and your passion will get stronger, like a plant you've kept in the closet that's finally getting some sun. Do it long enough and you will run smack into some of your biggest fears, which leads to the second key ritual for a balanced life.

Ritual 2: Forget "No Fear," Think "More Fear"

I always chuckle when I see T-shirts or other articles of clothing with the "no fear" motto on them. What they should say is "no worries," but I guess that was already taken as an Australian saying when the marketers got to it. At any rate, we seem to have this terrible aversion to fear, as though it is some kind of special emotion that must be avoided at all costs (by contrast, we don't seem to have any problem expressing our anger while driving the morning commute). In fact, I've found that fear is a great ally and mostly toothless. Let me see if I can convince you why, and also convince you that fear forms the basis of another incredibly useful work-life balancing ritual.

Play the following game with yourself: whenever a fear surfaces, instead of avoiding it, try to see how *quickly* you can address it. Run straight at it, the faster the better. Make a note of when you are first aware of whatever it is that is bugging you, and see if you can beat your personal best time between when you first noticed the fear and when you have plunged yourself into the heart of dealing with it.

Sound crazy? It should. Most of us avoid fear like the plague. I suppose that makes a certain sense; after all, if you were afraid of heights you wouldn't want to start playing around at the edge of cliff sides. And I suppose fear can be nature's way of telling you to keep a low profile (as in don't go piss off that guy holding the automatic weapon). But from a work-life balance perspective, fear is almost always a ball-and-chain holding us back. Let me explain why this ritual of running at your fears works and why it's such a powerful ally in keeping yourself balanced.

Start with the first ritual: quiet time. What do you think is going to happen after you've been giving yourself quiet time on a regular basis? Your passions will surface, and quickly on the heels of your passions will be fear. It will surface as one or more rock solid reasons showing you why pursuing your passion is impossible. "I can't do that" you might say "because I could never make enough money doing it." It's as if we all believe there is only one way to do a thing, only one channel for making it happen. We get some fixed idea in our heads about how things work and we take it to mean there is literally only one way to do that thing. We never entertain the notion that we might be able to draw upon our own creativity to make something happen in a different way. So you want to open that golf shop but figure you could never get the funding? No way you could afford to live on that kind of income? Well, take a look at it from a fresh angle. Why do you have to open a shop? What is it you really like about golf anyway? Are you absolutely sure there is no way to do it some other way? Maybe part time? Maybe as a volunteer? Help out with the local high school team? If you think about it long enough, the idea will hit you of how you can make it happen and still meet the other commitments in your life.

The details don't matter. If you give yourself regular quiet time, and if you even make half an attempt to live without blame, you won't be able to hide from the obvious. You will see your passion and you will see that it is within your grasp. And that's when the fear will come in, like the elephant in the room nobody wants to talk about. I promise you it will be there because if you weren't afraid of something, you would have done this thing you want to do long ago. Whatever you are afraid of has kept you from it, and you've invented a hundred ways to avoid thinking about it (like, oh, having that blackberry sewn to your hip and convincing yourself that you absolutely must be available 24x7 so that you have a constant stream of interruptions which ensure you'll never get enough quiet time to know what you are really passionate about).

This is where moving as fast as you can *towards the fear* comes in as a key ritual. Fear always follows the same pattern. It has a "phantom barrier" kind of effect— something that starts out looking like a brick wall but ends up completely insubstantial. Once you finally get yourself to take the plunge, and confront the fear, you realize that it was just a feeling after all and nowhere near as bad as you had imagined it would be. That "brick wall," the thing that you were so afraid of doing, looks completely different from the other side once you have faced the fear. "Gee" you find yourself saying "I was scared out of my mind, but it really wasn't so bad after all. I guess I didn't need to get so worked up about it."

Diving straight into the situation where you know you will be afraid, and doing it as quickly as you can, also has a very practical side effect: it is the most efficient way to get past the barriers that keep you from doing what you want. Your fears are there and they are keeping you from even getting started on what you really want from life. There is no denying it; they are in your way and the only way forward is to go through them. Following this ritual will make a game out of confronting fear, which will take some of the edge off what you are doing. It will also get you out of trying to "figure out" how best to address the fear, which is often just another form of stalling. Don't worry about being graceful, just go ahead and be afraid and do it anyway. Go ahead and fail if you have to—but whatever you do, *go ahead.* Be afraid; just as you are sometimes able to be angry, or to be happy or to be sad. Allow yourself to live with the emotion (fear is just a feeling, after all) and take whatever action is triggering that fear. No matter what happens you will be guaranteed of one thing: you will break through that barrier and you will experience that "gee, it wasn't so bad after all" feeling. And *that* is huge because it means you will have taken a big bite out of that phantom barrier. Next time, it will be easier. The more often you do this, the easier it will get until what started out as an impossibly high mountain of a barrier has become a speed bump you can take at will.

Ritual 3: Coach and Be Coached

All this discussion about the effects of the herd instinct begs a question: if herds are so powerful, why not create your own? They reinforce behavior, right? So why not create your own herd to keep pushing you in the direction you want to go? Hey, what a great idea!

In fact, people do this kind of thing all the time. They find someone that will go with them to the gym with to keep them honest about sticking to a workout routine. They join running clubs to train for a marathon. I've read studies that show you will literally gain more muscle and gain it faster if you have a workout buddy. So the idea of building a support group to keep you motivated is nothing new. It's such an obviously useful ritual it almost doesn't bear mentioning, except for a few details I have found to be highly useful.

First, you must form some kind of regular encouragement network, *which meets on a regular basis*, to keep yourself balanced. So much of our culture is anti-balance and messed up that it's virtually impossible to keep yourself in a healthy lifestyle without someone you can talk to regularly about whatever hurdles you are facing at the moment. You will be getting regular negative feedback from your culture, so it stands to reason you will need regular positive reinforcement. I've found that having weekly reinforcement is about right. When I interact with my close friends, or with my mentor, I try never go more than a two-week period without "checking in" with one of these "coaches" to receive a shot in the arm.

Note that you don't have to have a single coach, and a coach doesn't have to be doing exactly the same things you are doing. You can, for example, meet someone at the gym and do completely different activities. My wife and I did this for many years before we had children. We'd meet at the gym after work, she'd do her aerobics and I'd go for a run. We didn't actually spend any time together at the gym, but it kept me running on a regular basis. The distinction is important because it allows you to build a support group around work-life balancing issues which can be different for everyone. It allows me, for instance, to call my Mom regularly and talk with her, encourage her, and hear her encouragement of me as well, even though we are at completely different stages in life. I might be wrestling with how I'm going to save enough for retirement while she is wrestling with how to spend her retirement, but the principles are still the same: how to know what really matters, how to stay the course, how to face your fears.

Second, you will need to select people who are *outside of your work and family structure.* Your best bet is to pick somebody who is "neutral" about what you do for a living and what you do at home. Your friends are a great source.

121

They don't have to like you, they *choose* to like you, and they aren't family and they aren't trying to curry favor with you to improve their chances of a promotion. Their input comes from a neutral point of view which makes it more believable. They will be most likely to give you honest feedback. Give them a copy of this book and tell them you want their opinion. It doesn't have to be some big, heavy, bear-your-soul kind of thing, just let them know that you are working on trying to get a better handle on balancing your life, and you would value their honest feedback. When you meet for lunch or working out or Tuesday night poker, you can bring up whatever balance issue is on your mind at the time and get their input. If you do this on a regular basis, it doesn't have to be a big heavy thing, not some four-hour intervention session. Just "hey, I've got this thing on my mind that's currently eating my lunch...what's your take?" It doesn't have to be intense if the feedback is *regular*. And remember, from our chapter on process, that you also don't need to expect a solution all at once either. If you don't crack the nut today, maybe you will next week. Consistency is the key. Most of us don't want to sit around and have long, drawn-out, heart-to-hearts. So don't set yourself up for it. But don't let the issue fester, either; get regular feedback in bite-sized chunks.

Now, I need to include one word of caution here. The theory sounds great: talk to your friends, find someone who thinks that work-life balancing is important, and get them to give you feedback on a regular basis (by the way, you might consider returning the favor as well). But there is one big snag that you could hit. Some of the people who are closest to you, including your closest friends, may turn out to be the *worst* people for keeping you on track. When you share your thoughts and struggles about work-life balancing with them, you may find them telling you what you are trying to do is impossible. "That book you gave me on work-life balancing was full of it," they might say, "That bit about passion isn't reality—shoot, that don't pay the bills—and all that 'living without blame' stuff sounded like a load of psycho-babble to me. You know the saying: life's a bitch and then you die. Give it up, man."

If this happens, don't let it discourage you. Some of this is to be expected; after all, you are doing something that takes courage and many of your friends may secretly wish they had the strength to do what you are doing. But that would take courage on their part, and they may not be in a place to admit they lack the courage to try. This isn't a statement of intelligence or maturity here; even the most educated, most articulate, most high-powered executives can feel completely threatened by the work-life balancing issue. In fact, the more high-powered they are, the more they may have invested in a non-balanced lifestyle. Having the guts to balance your life isn't about maturity or intelligence; it's about having the courage to stand up to your culture. Even the smartest most "successful" people can lack courage. Misery loves company, as they say, and those who are miserable with their own work-life balance will want you to stay miserable with them (moo, moo—I hear the herd again). Watching you do something about getting your life together, when theirs is still messed up...well, let's just say they may not be so eager to watch that.

So you may have to search a bit to find someone open minded enough to encourage you. Keep searching until you find those people, and then cling to them. They will be your life preserver when you are at sea. They will help you get back on track when you stumble.

Once you've lined up your own coaches, you should also find someone whom *you* can coach. I would highly recommend you set aside time to *be a mentor to someone else who is working on work-life balancing.* That's right; take the time to teach someone else how to balance their life. It doesn't have to be a lot of time. I mentor three people whom I meet with once every two weeks for about an hour. Not much time at all, and I can usually fit it into my lunch hour, so there is no impact on my day. Mentoring someone else on how to balance their life will help you stay focused on balancing your own life. The reason this works is the same reason why the old medical school education technique works so well for training doctors. Traditional medical training involved three phases, "watch one," "do one," and then *"teach one."* You were not a fully trained doctor until you had mastered the technique yourself *and* trained someone else as well.

Don't worry about not being a "work-life expert." Good grief, nobody is an expert; we're all struggling with how to come to grips with modern life. It is the act of struggling itself which gives us the expertise that qualifies us to teach others. Mentoring someone else will give you the opportunity to support your own balance issues by forcing you to articulate what you are trying to do for yourself. When you find the words to help someone else successfully balance their lives, you will have found the same words to help yourself. By coaching others you will coach yourself. I cannot begin to tell you the number of times I have found myself dishing out advice to someone with a wry smile on my face, knowing I am telling them exactly what I myself need to be doing. Mentoring others will give you a laboratory to work through your ideas, a "neutral" setting where the problems are not yours, but someone else's, and where you can afford to be detached and focused on what is right versus what is scary or uncomfortable.

Ritual 4: Celebrate the Small Wins

Finally, make sure you celebrate your new, balanced lifestyle. Celebrate it a lot. Use any progress you make as an excuse to pop a cork and toast yourself. I literally keep a set of champagne splits (the small bottles) next to the beer in the fridge, and I pop one whenever I pluck up the courage to do something I've been meaning to do to get my life more in balance. For instance, tonight my daughter has her first kickball game and I'm going to have to leave work early to be there. It's going to feel awkward to walk out before everyone else. But tonight, after the game, I'll pop a cork to celebrate that I kept that commitment to my daughter. Remember ritual 2, running straight at your fears? Any time you face one of those it's a win you should celebrate. I even celebrate getting back on track after falling off the wagon, like when I finally started lifting weights again after a six month hiatus. I am totally shameless about it. No excuse is too small; as long as it is real evidence of the life I want to live, I'll give myself a pat on the back.

Why all the rah-rah? Isn't it overdone? No, not at all. And I'm not talking about a party-til-you-drop blowout every time you manage to pick your kid up from school on time. I'm talking about habit and positive reinforcement. It's the same thing as the difference between process and results that we covered in Chapter 1. We all know how to celebrate big things like graduation which are the *results*. But what about celebrating the *process* to get there? It can be long and difficult. In fact, if you are doing something counter-culture, like living a balanced life, we know that it *will* be difficult. We know the culture around you will send you a lot of signals that will reinforce bad habits and push you off balance. You have to counteract this by celebrating your wins. If you don't do it, nobody else will. You will need that positive reinforcement to create your own momentum. More importantly, you will need it to "mark" the progress you've made as a memorable event in your mind. There's a reason why we have ceremonies like graduations, weddings, funerals, etc. They are the punctuation marks of life. They put structure to our experiences, setting them off in chunks we can remember. If you are going to create a new lifestyle, you need that structure to create building blocks for your new life.

You need to be able to remember your wins to build momentum around your balanced lifestyle. You are creating a new habit, and it will go against years of negative training. My Dad had a favorite saying he would trot out whenever I'd come to him with some difficult problem. "Do you know how to eat an elephant?" he'd ask. "One bite at a time." Restructuring your life to make it more balanced can be like eating an elephant. It can seem like forever before you reach any results worth a formal celebration. But remember, what we are talking about here is more than a result; it's an ongoing habit pattern, so it's important to celebrate the habit. Celebration, with some kind of simple ceremony, will help you create a cognitive structure where the wins will stick out in your mind. You'll be able to say to yourself "oh yeah, I remember how that used to scared the crap out of me, but I've stood up to it before and it wasn't so bad. I can do it again." Without some regular celebration ritual, you will get discouraged, you will forget your successes, and it will be easy to sink back into your old habits. You are building momentum, rebuilding your own internal positive history to counteract

126

years of negative history. Use ceremony to fix your new life into your mind. It's the only way you will be able to break away from the old habits.

Rituals 5 and 6: The "Sometimes Rituals"

In the first edition of this book, I did not include these next two rituals. They were, it seemed to me, obvious from the rest of the text, and I felt like I had already overloaded my readers with enough to keep them busy. Moreover, I'm not a fan of "checklist solutions" in any form, and I am very reluctant to suggest anything that smacks of a formulaic, one-size-fits-all solution. Yet, as I have coached executives and others over the years, I've found that these two rituals are particularly useful in certain situations where people get bogged down trying to put work-life balancing into practice. These, then, are my "sometimes rituals," a couple of tricks I find that I use on an as-needed basis (not always regularly, as with the other four rituals) to help get me out of a jam.

Ritual 5: The Walk Through

First, let me paint a picture of the situation. There you are, chugging along quite nicely, feeling pretty good about yourself. You've got your life more balanced, you're taking some quiet time on a regular basis, and you've begun to unearth some long-held passions. Recently, you've struck up the courage to take on one of those passions and see whether you can make some progress. You take some initial actions, start to gather some data to make a plan, and you are even taking time to celebrate your initiative and give yourself credit for finally doing that thing you've told yourself for years you should do, but just never quite got around to doing. In short, you are riding a work-life balancing high.

And then one day it happens. You wake up and realize you are frustrated. You realize it's been several days or even several weeks and you haven't gotten anywhere. What seemed to be going well only a few short weeks ago now seems to be going nowhere. It would make you angry if it weren't for the fact that you are dumbfounded about how you could so quickly get stuck when only a short while ago the path ahead seemed so obvious. You have the hard evidence right before your eyes, your own version of my champagne corks, little mementoes from your celebrations of the progress you were making. And you haven't changed anything you can think of; you are still taking quiet time, still running straight at your fears, still engaged in coaching and being coached. But it's clear you are stuck and you can't figure out why.

And it may be that even on some academic level, you understand the basic problem. You recognize the situation as a kind of blame game. Clearly you are "blocking" yourself, somehow telling yourself there are obstacles in your way, filling your time with the equivalent of "I can't" messages that are preventing your next move. But even if you do get this far, even if you do realize you are stuck in some kind of blame-game tar pit, it doesn't mean you know how to break free. And even if you have a coach to help you talk things over, he or she may not be able to provide much help if you don't have some method for systematically breaking down the situation to get at the blame, expose it, and show it for what it is.

This is where the "walk through" technique comes in. What you are experiencing is a kind of blurring of the real and the unreal. You are hitting up against an assumption that is so strong, so fundamental, that you cannot see it for what it is. It is something you have been assuming for so long that you no longer recognize it as an assumption but instead take it as fact. It is "unreal" but you believe it to be real and thus you can't see it as a kind of blame. Moreover, because it is so fundamental, it never sticks out during your quiet time, and it never occurs to you to bring it up during your conversations with your coach(es). It is like trying to remember how you learned to walk; it happened so long ago and is now so much a part of what you do that it is impossible to break it back down to its basic parts.

An example will help to clarify. I was coaching someone once who was struggling with how to get through all the email he was receiving. It seemed to him like it was a mountain of email, and that it never let up. The emails came in and he needed to reply in a timely fashion. He tried every trick he could think of, but he really had no control over the flow of email, and there is a limit to how fast one can type. It was eating up all his time and he was totally frustrated with what felt like his inability to remove this obstacle so that he could make progress on other parts of his job that he was much more excited about doing.

And so I introduced him to the concept of a "walk through." Walk throughs are a standard practice among computer programmers, used as a technique for capturing software "bugs" (errors in computer programs) before code is released as a product. I'm not sure of the exact statistics here, but some incredibly high number (like 70%) of software bugs can be found using walk throughs. Here's the way they work. The programmer who has written the code (the author) makes a paper printout of the code which he or she hands out to several other programmers who will help with the walk through. These other programmers (the participants) are typically selected because they are not overly familiar with the code. They are competent programmers in their own right and they certainly know programming, but they bring their own, outside perspectives which are unbiased about any design choices which may have been made in the development of the code. The author explains the general problem he or she was trying to solve, and then proceeds to walk through the program itself, line by line, explaining the choices that were made as the program was devised. The participants can interject at any time asking "why?" questions, as in "why did you do this" or "why did you make that choice" or, most importantly, *"why did you make that assumption?"* What these other programmers are doing, of course, is forcing the author to rethink the most important decisions that went in to the design of the program, separating out what is a true constraint from what was simply a design choice. This often helps the author see other options to simplify the code, avoid traps, or otherwise make the program more robust.

Can you see the overlaps to work-life balancing here? Even the language overlaps. One can characterize our own thinking as "programming" we have received through inputs from our past, our culture, the herd, whatever. We are the "authors" of our own programs, fundamentally able to change our "code," and doing the best we can with whatever resources we have. We have to make choices, and many times we do so without complete knowledge of a situation. We don't have unlimited time or assets, so we sometimes are forced to borrow whatever works, from whatever sources we have. We don't get to pick our parents, our childhoods, or the cultural biases into which we are thrust. And as a consequence, we end up with tons of assumptions embedded in our "programs" that seem like hard constraints but are, in fact, just assumptions. But we are so close to the "code" we can't tell the assumptions from the truths, even if we stare at the program until our eyes glaze over. We need other "programmers" to listen to us explain our logic and stop us when we state something as a fact which is really not fact at all.

The beauty of a walk through is that it gives you a formal structure for getting at deeply embedded blame language. It gives you a simple way of taking a knotty problem and chipping away at it without getting your feelings hurt, without having to figure it out all in one go, and without having to burden your listener with the expectation of them coming up with some brilliant insight to solve all the mysteries of your life. All you have to do is say "hey, listen, I have something that has been bugging me, and I just need someone to listen to me for 15 minutes and tell me where I'm making assumptions. Just listen and tell me where you think I'm nuts or where you'd do things differently." And all they have to do is listen and give you their perspective. They don't have to be an expert, they just have to be different, and everybody has a different perspective.

Here's the beautiful thing: even if your listeners don't provide any direct solutions (and most often they do not), just hearing where they question your "programming" will provide you with clues to where you are making your assumptions. Most of the time they will say something like "Wow, well that's not the way I do it. I usually do so-and-so" and then you are off to the races comparing how you take different approaches, what you each consider "fact" versus what can be changed. By listening to you explain how you wrote your "program," and having them share with you how they have written theirs, they expose options for situations you would otherwise never think of as optional. They help you expose the assumptions that are propping up your blame game.

Coming back to my example, when we did a walk through with my email sufferer, John, we found he was making a huge assumption about the speed of his email responses. He felt his responses needed to be prompt, that every email had to be answered within a few hours of its receipt. He felt strongly that this was particularly true of emails he received from his boss. Had he ever asked his boss if this was, in fact, true? No, but he was sure (see the assumption?) that his boss would say yes. When he was feeling particularly overloaded, had he ever considered responding to an email by asking the sender when they actually required a response? No, again, he had simply assumed that everyone wanted a rapid reply. And finally, had he ever considered the fact that when it came to his responses, quality might be more important than quickness? Had he considered that he might do more for himself, and more for his company, by only replying when he felt he had something of value to add, versus answering quickly and thereby generating more email that everyone else had to read? Would it not be better to establish a reputation for writing emails that were really on point, versus simply writing emails that were on time? Which reputation would he prefer to have: would he want people saying "Wow, it's an email from John and he always writes good stuff, I'd better read it" or would he want people saying "Oh good grief, another email from John to go with the 15 other emails I got from him today; I think I'll leave it until later."

John tells me now that he feels like his email load has been cut in half if not more. He sets aside two times a day to answer emails and ignores it the rest of the day, unless he gets something urgent. When he is unsure of the required time for a reply he simply asks, and when he must reply quickly but feels he could generate a better response if given more time, he says so and thereby gives his reader a choice to get something better than his quick reply. In short, by challenging his assumptions and focusing on what he can do well, he is now in control of his email instead of it being in control of him. He hasn't sacrificed any quality nor has he hurt his reputation at work; in fact, quite the opposite is true. All he has done is transition from an "I can't" (as in "I can't stand my email") to an "I want" (as in "I want to find a way to spend more time on other work") by developing a new process for communicating his needs more directly to others, so he can meet both his needs and theirs. All of this was possible because our walk through exposed some deeply held assumptions he was unaware he was making. Once he saw them for what they were, he already had all the tools he needed to craft a solution that worked for him.

Walk thoughts are a simple structure that can yield powerful results. You only need to satisfy two requirements: an author who is willing to go step-by-step through what they are doing, attempting as much as possible to explain their justifications behind why they do what they do, and at least one listener who is focused on questioning those justifications that appear odd to them. The trick is to stay away from trying to find solutions. It is far more important to focus on the questioning, to expose all the assumptions in the justifications and separate them from fact. Solutions will present themselves to the author once he or she sees the key assumptions that are gumming up the works.

Note that it is possible to alter the formula for a walk through based on your circumstances. For example, you can use multiple simultaneous listeners instead of just one to great effect. Often times a group of people, each with a different perspective, will expose many more assumptions than a single listener, and sometimes the group of listeners will build on each other's suggestions to provide some very interesting alternatives. Another trick I've used is to play the role of both author and listener when I have no listener available. This can be a great way to structure your own quiet time. For example, you can spend, say, 20 minutes using a recorder to tape yourself explaining all the reasons why some issue is currently giving you grief. Go ahead and vent, blaming everything in sight that you think is holding you back. Then put the recorder down for 10 minutes, get a cup of coffee, and let yourself settle down. Now play back your rant, paying particular care to listen for anything that smacks of being unreasonable. You'll be amazed at how different something sounds when you hear it, versus what you thought it sounded like when you were saying it.

Ritual 6: The Rule of Judgment

My second "sometimes ritual" is a rule I find comes in handy when I sense I will have to weather a particularly strong storm of peer pressure. I call it "The Rule of Judgment" and it's something I coach people on all the time. It's a popular topic around the holiday time of year because that's when so many of us spend extended time with family in close (cramped?) quarters that would test the limits of our tolerance at the best of times. But it works any time you are feeling center stage, when it seems like everyone is looking at you and passing judgment on you, when you feel like you just won't be able to live up to those expectations you are convinced everyone else has placed upon you.

The rule is simple. It goes like this:

*Practice actively judging everyone, most importantly yourself, **only** by whether or not they (you) are taking actions to make their (your) life what they (you) truly want it to be.*

This little rule works like magic. It keeps you from getting frustrated by what other people say or do, and it gives you a way to interact without setting people off (and sending Uncle Bob or Aunt Sadie into a screaming temper fit).

Let me explain why this works. It all revolves around what I call the "gallery" effect. Think golf for a moment (yeah, here comes another sports analogy). If you have ever watched a golf match, then you will know what I mean by the "gallery." It is the massive throng of people that swarms around the course, following the favorite players, "ooh-ing" and "ahh-ing" over every shot. There's nothing else quite like it in the world of sport. Imagine for a moment that you are Tiger Woods (yes, I know, it's a stretch for me too, but one can dream). Everywhere you go, thousands of people flock to ogle at your every little move. You can't do anything without literally thousands of pairs of eyeballs watching you. It's a palpable force, flowing like a sea all around you, whispering about you just out of ear shot, growing suddenly and ringingly silent right before you hit your shots. It is a living thing that you can never get away from, that will always be there watching you, judging your every move.

Now, we all make judgments all the time. We have to or we'd die. We have to drive on the road, judging what others will do. We have to make purchases at the store, picking based on price or quality or whatever other feature we want or need. Judgment is a natural part of being human, and it becomes a habit (as it must) that we instantly and unconsciously engage to navigate the complexities of the world around us. If you didn't constantly make judgments, you wouldn't be able to get out of bed.

But when it comes to judging each other, we don't like to admit that we do it. It feels wrong (and is wrong, in many ways) to judge people. Is someone better or worse because of their religion or the color of their skin? Of course not, and we work hard to avoid such judgments.

Yet, we still do judge each other, and I think it happens in particularly strong doses at the holiday season. Did I get the present I wanted? Did she like the present I bought? I only see him once a year at this time, so I have to make the most of it. I love her so much I can't tell her what I really think. You know the drill...we all do.

And this brings me back to the gallery effect. Certain times, like the holidays, can feel like playing a game of golf, where every tiny shot is watched by the "gallery" of people around you. It's like you are suddenly immersed in our own "match play" game of golf, with a thronging gallery following you around, watching and evaluating every little thing you do. At holiday time, it's a big deal because it is family, and we do love them, and despite how much we might not like to admit it, we do want them to love us back. But it can happen at other times, like when we have to make a big presentation at work, or when show up at a party and feel under dressed, or any time we feel we are center stage with an audience whose opinions of us matter to us.

The good news is you can avoid the gallery effect. The weird thing is that the way to do it is not to avoid judgment, which would seem to be the obvious thing, but instead to *actively practice judgment.* Yep, that's right...go ahead and judge and do it on purpose! That is the key to having a good time with judgment.

Why does this work? Partly, it's because trying to deny judgment is like Tiger Woods trying to say "hey folks, can't you all just walk away and leave me in peace?" Sounds nice in theory, but it's just not going to happen. And expecting to be around family or close friends or coworkers and not be subject to judgment is just as unlikely. But—and this is the key—you don't have to play by the typical rules of judgment. You can define your own rules, which is where the "Rule of Judgment" I outlined above comes in.

The idea is to change the effects of judgment by *changing how you think about it and how you engage in it.* The nature of judgment, after all, is that it is based on some relative standard. Once you realize that there are typically multiple different standards for any given judgment, you can grasp how it's possible to control the situation by picking the standard you will use. For example, if you are buying a car, you can judge it in any of a number of ways. You can judge it on price, and go for the lowest cost. You can judge it on the ride and go for the most comfort. You can judge it on mileage and go for the best miles-per-gallon rating. You can judge it on quality and go for the fewest repairs. You can judge it on beauty or perceived status. Hey, when I was 22 and single and living in Houston and wishing I could be a chick magnet, you can bet the reason I bought that mustang convertible had a whole lot more to do with how I thought I looked while I was driving around than how much money I could save!

So judgment is not absolute. It is arbitrary (hmm, sounds like the herd again, doesn't it?) which means *you* can select the scale against which everything will be measured. You can set the standard rather than having it set for you. And I have found that my little rule of judgment works great both as a way to do the judging and as a way to listen to the judgments being made of you.

Let me give you two concrete examples.

First, let us imagine you are talking to your sister Mary. You ask Mary what she has been up to lately, and she says she is thinking about buying a new car. Now, you know Mary and she always seems to go for those kinds of cars you think are awful, because you are a granola-head and you think everyone should buy small cars that don't spew a ton of greenhouse gases into our overly burdened atmosphere. Mary, on the other hand, loves her big cars and drives around in her Lincoln Extensus, which needs its own zip code for a parking spot. Typically (that is, if you were not following the rule of judgment) you would feel your hackles going up, because you can see yourself getting into another predictable argument with Mary, fruitlessly trying to convince her to see the horrible effects of her gluttony, while she dons that insipid smile you hate so much, looking pityingly at you because you squeeze yourself into the equivalent of a golf cart with a roof every day. Obviously, the conversation is not going to go well.

However, imagine instead that you employ the rule of judgment to navigate this conversation differently than the automatic train wreck outlined above. Instead of judging Mary on what *you* think should make her happy, you instead engage her in a conversation about what truly makes *her* happy. "Oh really," you say, "that sounds great, Mary. What are you looking for in your next car? I always feel like there are so many choices it makes my head spin. What are, say, the five things that you really feel like you must have in your next car?" Now, you see, you are opening a door to enter into a conversation with Mary about what really matters to her, what she really cares about. You are inviting her to talk about her car purchase not by some arbitrary, defined-by-the-herd standard, but by what she cares most about. Who knows, she might even confide that she has always been a bit afraid of driving on a road full of cars, which is why she likes a big car, but she hates the fact that the only way to get the room she really wants in a car is to end up polluting more and spending $50 at the pump every week to fill the tank. You could end up having a great conversation debating alternatives she could consider to get what she wants. And if you listen very carefully, you might even hear her talk about the difference between what she really wants and what she thinks she is supposed to want. It may be that she feels like the only way to keep up with everyone in her neighborhood is to buy a Lexus, yet she secretly would love to stick with the car she has and spend the money on something else. By listening for what she *truly* wants, and judging her *only* by whether she is taking actions that match her desires, you can not only have a conversation that won't set her off, you might find a new depth of closeness.

As a second example, imagine you are in your mid forties and thinking about a career change. You are talking with your brother Frank who is one of those "know it all guys." He has an expert opinion at the ready on every topic, and he can whip it out and present it with what sounds like absolute authority in a booming voice that could drown out a chorus of opera singers. He's your brother, and you love him, but it chaps your hide that he can be so rigidly certain about everything. Against your better instincts, you tell him that despite the fact that you've been an engineer for 20 years, you are considering going back to law school and starting up a practice in family law with an emphasis on divorce cases, something you've recently discovered is your new passion (alright, so I'm taking a little poetic license here; just go with me for the story, ok?). Frank, alias "authority man," pipes up right away and says "you don't want to do that. What you really need to do is go into patent law. With your engineering background, you'd be a perfect fit, and be making the big bucks right out of law school. Law firms would roll out the red carpet because of your background. Nobody is going to think a propeller head like you has any place in a divorce proceeding." Of course, you stopped listening right after he said "you don't want to do that..." out of sheer annoyance that he'd have the audacity to think he knew what was best for you. By the time he got to "propeller head" your blood pressure had gone up by 20% and you were considering the best way to tell him off.

Now, once again, consider our "Rule of Judgment" and ask yourself one simple question: was Frank judging you by that rule? Was he listening for what you truly wanted and judging you by whether you were taking the actions to reach your goal? Absolutely not. He broke that rule with the first six words out of his mouth. And notice this, by breaking the rule *he wasn't talking about you at all!* He was, in fact, talking about himself and everything he said actually had nothing to do with you. Reread his comments and you will see what he is talking about is really *his* strategy for what *he* thinks *he* would do to make money as a lawyer if *he* were an engineer. He didn't ask one question nor make a single remark about you. He didn't ask whether this was truly something you wanted, nor did he ask how you felt about switching from something you'd been doing for 20 years to something totally new. Not one question came up about what had caused your change of heart to a field that seemed so different, nor did he ask how you had come to such a profound shift in your own thinking. Those would have been positive judgments, engaging questions, around which you could have had a great conversation.

But being aware of the Rule of Judgment, you know better. At this point you now have a choice. You can simply say "well thanks for the advice, Frank. I'll give it some thought. By the way, whom do you favor in the Super Bowl?" and change the subject. Or you could say "I know, I know. It seems wild, doesn't it? I mean, it's so different from what I've been doing for 20 years, and it was amazing how I came to the realization. I'd be happy to share that with you, it's an interesting story" and see if he bites. Either way, you are putting the conversation into your own terms, using your own rules.

Give it a try. Try listening to what people say they want and encouraging them to take actions that move them closer to their goals. And when you are lying awake on that sleepless night before some big presentation, try judging yourself not by how you think everyone might react, but instead on whether you are doing what you want to be doing and taking the actions to make your presentation as fun for yourself as you can make it. See if this kind of approach doesn't change your perspective, make it more fun to engage in conversations with people who matter to you, and give you a whole new way to feel good about what you are doing, stop wringing your hands, and get back to a place where you can relax and get some sleep.

That covers the rituals I recommend for staying in balance. Four of them are habits I strongly suggest you practice on a regular basis; two are for use as the situation merits. And I'll say once again that these rituals will be easy to ignore because they seem so mundane. It can seem silly to take an hour a day for quiet time, especially when you are feeling pushed to get more and more done. When your schedule is crammed full of meetings in the crush to meet a deadline, it is tempting to cancel coaching or mentoring meetings to buy yourself more time. But consider this before you drop out of doing the rituals I've outlined above. Work-life balancing is not rocket science. It amounts to little more than taking the time to do what you already know you need to do. It takes no special training beyond being able to handle a calendar. Anyone with two brain cells and a synapse can do it. And yet, the vast majority of people today feel out of balance. Which begs a question: why, if work-life balancing is so simple are so many people struggling with it? Why has it been a topic on the over of every major business publication over the past two years? The answer is because while it is *simple*, it is not *easy*. As we've learned here, the world itself is out of balance, and we live in a culture that constantly pushes you off balance. The habits of the herd are always there, relentlessly dragging you in the wrong direction. You must have some way to push back, to have something counteracting the negative pull with positive reinforcement. You will need habits to shore up your resolve because you can bet the world will always be there trying to chip it away.

Story: Sticking Out and The Spare Tire

I'll give you a perfect example of why trying to live in balance can make you feel like you stick out. It's a little story about my waist line. I've been trying to lose that pesky ten pounds that seems to settle about a man's middle once he passes 30. The dreaded "spare tire." Naturally, I've been thinking about the kinds of things I eat, and it suddenly struck me that *I have never taken the time to think about what I would call "good" food.* I'm not talking about good for you, as in some kind of boring dried up bran flakes that scrape as they go down. I'm talking about the food *I* consider good, not all the imperfect junk loaded up with salt, chemicals, and God knows what else that the fast-food industry pushes on us. Have you ever tasted a red grapefruit from the Texas Rio Grande Valley? They are so sweet they don't even need sugar…just cut and eat. Have you ever had freshly picked corn on the cob from a Midwestern farm? Nothing like it. There is a ton of great stuff to eat out there, if I just spend five minutes thinking about it. Why did I ever think that something from a fast-food burger joint could pass for good food when there is a sushi joint right next door that will give me something far better in less time?

The point is I never really thought about it at all. It was just what was there in front of me and I, quite literally, swallowed the marketing messages without thinking about it. In truth, there is absolutely no reason to eat junk food. None. I don't buy the convenience argument either, because I can tell you when I am in a hurry to eat something, it is truly wonderful to be able to pull a grapefruit out of the fridge, cut it open, and eat it. Or to grab a banana, for that matter, which comes in its own convenient to-go wrapper. Nature's own fast-food.

If I'm going to eat something I want it to be good. My definition of good. And for me, right now, that means real food without all the added preservatives. I want it to be fresh, not loaded up with salt because some lazy fast-food company is trying to cover up for the fact that it can't be bothered to try to deliver quality and freshness at the same time. And if I am going to go on a binge and eat whatever gets put on the plate, then I want to do it with my wife, at a really nice restaurant, with great service and a good bottle of wine and some good background music. But I digress.

However, here's the rub. It's going to be strange for me to have the discipline to eat my "good food." I'm going to stand out. A case in point: birthday parties for my kids often serve pizza. Guess what? It's usually something awful from one of the usual pizza chains. We all stand around eating this junk, and then I wonder why I can't lose that pesky ten pounds. In fact, *I've* planned my *own* daughters' birthdays to include this salt-ridden, let's-see-how-high-we-can-get-our-blood-pressure kind of chain pizza. Why have I done that? I mean, cake and ice cream is a long standing tradition, but who ever said the rest of the food had to be a medical risk? It's clearly an instance of me just following the crowd without thinking.

Now don't get me wrong. I am not on some high holy crusade against fast food. I'm not into more government regulation and I don't want to be the food police for my neighbors. I am totally happy for people to eat whatever they want. Hey, maybe you happen to come from a long line of pizzeria owners and for you pizza *is* a birthday family tradition. I'm not suggesting that people suddenly go out and start torching pizza-joints. That would just be

144

another arbitrary shift in direction of the herd. And I've been to plenty of birthday parties where the parents *have* thought ahead an provided an easy alternative to pizza by buying one of those veggie plates you can get at virtually any grocery store. The point is that *I* don't have to eat fast food just because everyone else does, and I need to give myself permission to eat what I consider good food.

But I will stick out. Can't you just hear the reaction? "Hey Paul, what's the matter? You on some kind of girly diet or something? C'mon, we're having a contest to see how many slices of pizza we can eat in less than a minute. Don't wimp out on me, man." I'm exaggerating again, but you get my point. We live in herds. Herds set standards that are arbitrary. Balance is not arbitrary, it is deliberate. Put the two together and ultimately you will end up being forced to think differently. That means you will stick out. When you do, the herd will notice and, what's more, the herd will put *you* on notice. Someone will challenge your actions.

In these situations, what really works for me is to follow the Rule of Judgment and just "show my cards" so to speak. Just tell 'em what I'm doing. The key is not to be mean or spiteful. When anyone asks, all I say is that I've simply made a decision that I've had enough fast food in my life, and there are too many other tasty and healthy foods that I'm more interested in. That's it. No defensiveness or moralizing needed. Just a simple "gee that's very kind but no thanks, I've decided to eat something else." The amazing thing about this approach is the reaction I get. It's almost always something like "you know, I've thought about that too, but haven't been able to get past such-and-such" and then the conversation turns positive. It becomes more of a brainstorming session about

145

how to eat healthy food in a world that surrounds us with junk.

So, yeah, you're gonna stick out. But stick to your guns, don't be mean about it, and show your cards. Who knows, you might be surprised to find a lot of folks thinking the same way you are. And even if that doesn't happen, you will at least be doing what you want, instead of literally swallowing the party line.

Story: Buck the System, Make Friends

I'll let you in on a little secret about this book: this was the hardest chapter for me to write. When I set out on this project I promised myself I would strike a positive tone (ok, maybe a sprinkle of sarcasm here and there) but it was almost impossible to be positive in this chapter. It was so tempting to be bitter when writing about "the herd" and how it can make you feel left out. It would have been easy to turn this whole chapter into a giant bitch session, and I'm not entirely sure I've avoided descending to that level despite my efforts to avoid doing just that. Which is why this next story is my favorite. It's a story about how I joined one of the oldest, most rigid, most crufty herds around, went against the grain, and did it without offending everyone within a five mile radius. It's about attitude, and how to go against the grain without rubbing everyone the wrong way. It's a story that proves to me a lesson I have repeated to myself many times: going against the herd doesn't have to be destructive.

The setting is graduate school, with me as the graduate student. Now, one thing you need to know about graduate school is that it may well be the last vestige of medieval culture we have left in our society. There is no system more backward, more feudal, more like tolerated slavery than graduate Ph.D. work. When you are a graduate student, you are a surf, in thrall to your graduate advisor. Your work belongs completely to your advisor; separate from him or her and you separate from all your work. You have to start over from scratch. One makes one's academic name through the political connections of one's advisor, and the politics of the research world are the most intense I've seen anywhere. Unlike the business world where you have the option to go it alone and appeal to the market to prove your value, there is no way to go it alone in the academic world. There is no impartial judge like the market; everything is reputation-based. The only way to get your Ph.D. is to establish an acceptable reputation, and the only way to do that is to piggy back off of someone who will bring you along on their coat tails.

So you can imagine that going against the grain as a graduate student is about like jumping off a tall building; you can expect to run into something very solid very quickly. And yet, I was able to buck this system and to do it in a way that I came in for a soft landing. Probably this was due to the fact that some of the very best people I have ever met have been my graduate school advisors, and I suspect this is true of most academics. They may live and work in a backward, medieval system, but they are truly fantastic people open to new ways of thinking (which is their job, after all). And that's the beauty of this story; that you can appeal to this higher nature in people to get around "the system" without having to slash and burn everything in your path.

My first semester at graduate school I was a research assistant to one of the professors in the department. His name was Ben, and it was very gracious of him to take me on as a research assistant, in which capacity I wrote software to implement some of the ideas he was working on. Unfortunately, the topic Ben was pursuing was not something I wanted to study. I had my own ideas about the direction I wanted to take my research. So I was faced with a dilemma right off the bat: either work under Ben's direction and hitch my wagon to his wagon train hoping to eventually find my place on his extended team of graduate students with a topic I could claim as my own, or else confront him with what I really wanted to do and see if I could convince him to let me go my own way. The "normal" thing to do was the former: let you advisor set your path and follow dutifully along. But I knew that wasn't where my heart was. How could I possibly be successful forcing myself to pursue something when my passion lay in a completely different direction?

In short, I needed to buck the system. So I plucked up my courage and set up a time to meet with Ben to discuss what I wanted to do. I remember saying to him something like the following, "Ben, you're a great guy and I think the world of the work you are doing, but I really want to do something different." His reply was something very similar, as in "Paul, I think you are a great guy too, and I like your ideas, but my funding is for a very specific grant to address a very specific research topic. Bottom line, I'm not going to use these funds to pay you to do the research you want to do."

We had hit an impasse. He'd called my bluff, so to speak. The funding was his to control and he was completely within his rights to tell me he was going to set the direction of how the funding was to be spent. I remember thinking, as I sat in his office, that I'd hit a wall. "Oh my God," I thought "I have no choice. I have to suck it up and do what he wants because that's what's paying my salary right now and I have no other option. I'm going to have to do this for six more years, working on something where my heart really isn't in it. It's going to be a disaster."

And that's when it hit me how I could turn it all into a positive. I knew, even then, that my heart was not in the work I was doing for Ben. There was no way I could really do justice to Ben's research project. He needed someone who was really "into" the work. He did not need me taking up space (and funds), plodding along with "The System" and doing a mediocre job. Both he, and I, would be better served by working towards a situation where everyone's passions lined up with the work they were doing.

So I said to him, "Ben, you're right. You do need someone to work on this project as you have outlined it. I just don't think I am that person. And I don't think it is doing either of us a service for me to pretend that I am. Let's do this. I will stay on to the end of this semester and do the best possible job I can for you. In return, let's see if we can find someone to replace me. I'll bring them up to speed on what I've done and we will transition them into my spot. During that same period, would you be willing to advise me on what I should do to pursue my own research ideas?"

To make a long story short, that's exactly what we did. He was delighted to help me set up a strategy and I helped him find someone to take my spot on his team. We parted ways on great terms at the end of that semester, and I took out a loan to cover my income needs while I pursued research grants with other professors in the department. By the end of the next semester, I had landed a grant with another professor and started down my own path.

The best part about the story is that Ben remained both a good friend and a good advisor. When it came time for me to assemble a research committee of three professors "outside" my specific area of research, Ben was my first pick and he agreed right away. He continued to offer me good advice and great insights even in to my own research, which was not his area of specialty. In the end, we ended up as good friends and colleagues. The alternative would have been years of grudging work on my part, probably done poorly, with Ben having to hound me all the way. Clearly, bucking the system early on was the right thing to do.

You might think this is just one of those lucky situations with a gushy happy ending that doesn't represent reality. But I disagree. I think most people, the vast majority in fact, want to help others. I think they will go out of their way to help you pursue your goals if you approach them honestly and ask them to work with you to find a mutually beneficial situation. The key here was *my willingness to help Ben first*, to make sure his needs were addressed, and then ask for his help in return. My motives were positive for both myself and the system I was trying to work around. By making sure I addressed the key concerns of "The System" I was able to work around it, and also get others to help me work around it.

So you can buck the system without destroying it. It just takes some creative thinking and a willingness to give before you get. Best of all, if you take this approach, you will find you have willing advocates to help you.

Story: Run for the Border

Perhaps you've heard the phrase "a coming-to-Jesus meeting?" It refers to having a confrontation with someone, one-on-one, where you let the person know he or she has crossed a line. It's a reckoning, an accounting for behavior, and it's not easy. Nobody likes to have personal confrontations. We avoid them like we avoided the bully on the playground, but in so doing we make things much worse for ourselves because the situation festers. Eventually you must have the confrontation or you can't look yourself in the mirror. This is a story about how you can *purposely* use this kind of meeting to your advantage, to run *towards* something you're afraid of doing and get it behind you as quickly as possible (ritual 2). You can use it any time someone crosses a boundary, a border of what you consider good behavior. If you "run for the border" and have the confrontation, and do it as quickly as possible, it makes things a whole lot better.

I've had lot of jobs, and I've been on teams where new people join the team on a fairly frequent basis. I such a setting you often find yourself thrown together with others you don't know but with whom you must work. They are strangers and they can't possibly know every detail about how you like to work. The result is inevitable; someone is going to cross a line and do something that you are not happy about. You're going to have to "set them straight" which means confrontation.

Here's one that happened to me recently. One of my boundaries is that I like to be asked before someone promises something where I am the one who has to deliver. I don't like people committing me without consulting me, and yet this is exactly what happened to me in this story. We had a new person join our team. She was my peer, not my boss. She was enthusiastic about launching a program she had been charged with promoting. As part of that promotion, she needed a presentation on patents, and she found out that I was something of an expert on that topic.[16] So she proceeded to set up an orientation meeting, plan for me to make a presentation on patents, and then announced to the whole team during a team-wide call that I was going to give this patent presentation. The problem was, she had never spoken to me about it. Worse, to make an announcement on a call with the entire team participating put me in a spot where I felt awkward questioning her. For me to have said "hey, no I'm not!" would have made me look like I wasn't being a team player. She had simply assumed that since I was the best person for the job, that she could just unilaterally assign me the task. It made me feel like I was letting myself be bullied. Needless to say, I was not a happy camper. I knew something needed to be said, and the longer I let it ride, the worse it would get.

So what did I do? I called her and said I needed get about 15 minutes of her time to talk about something that was bugging me. She came by my office and I told her that I needed to clear the air on something. I told her that I valued my working relationship with her and wanted to keep it strong, but that something had happened which bothered me. I told her that it was not a huge deal, but that I believed in *nipping these things in the bud specifically when they are not a big deal* because, in my experience, it all works out better. After all, if something is bugging me

---

[16] For anyone interested in the topic, see my book *Reinventing Invention*, available at www.innovationmatters.com/publications.php

how would she know if I didn't tell her? I couldn't expect her to read my mind. I told her that when she had announced me giving a talk on patents in front of the whole team, without consulting me, that it bugged me. I told her I was very open to giving talks on patents, in fact, I enjoy public speaking; I just need to be asked. I told her all this one-on-one, without embarrassing her publicly.

The amazing thing—and this happens all the time—was how good the result turned out. She apologized, said she had no intention of putting me on the spot, and said she would definitely consult me in the future. I told her not to beat herself up about it, and just repeated my positive intent: that I realized she would have no way of reading my mind, that I wanted a good working relationship, and that I figured the best thing was to just be direct and let her know how to work with me. You could feel the tension disappear. You could hear the appreciation in her voice. She's not an idiot; she had sensed something was bugging me even if she wasn't sure what it was. Having the confrontation, quickly, in this positive setting, completely diffused a brewing situation. We've never had a problem since and we are, in fact, on very good working terms.

I've repeated this scene many times. Only once did I get a negative reaction from a guy who said, essentially, that I'd just better get used to it because that was how he was going to treat me and he didn't give a crap. Even that was a positive because at least I knew he was someone who was not going to be reasonable, so I had no compunction about working around him.

Confront early, do it in a positive way, and you save yourself a ton of grief. You also get to put something nasty behind you, which is just a much better way to live. Remember the friction and overhead we talked about in

Chapter 3? Having a confrontation early short circuits any time you would spend stewing about the issue. After all, how much of your time do you want to dedicate to bitching about someone else? Better by far, in my book, to clear the air and move on to the things I'm excited about.

Story: Celebrating a Sleepless Night

A close cousin of the last story comes in the form of a little cork I keep in with my collection of corks I've popped from champagne bottles celebrating events of significance in my life. The interesting thing about this cork is that it celebrates the night I was so scared out of my wits about an upcoming presentation that I kept myself up all night worrying. Strange thing to celebrate, eh?

I was on travel visiting IBM headquarters for the first time. The team I worked for gave annual "status reports" to the highest level executives in the company. It was our one time a year to shine in front of the people who mattered the most. These were the same people, by the way, that we relied upon for the funding that paid our salaries. I had been talking to my boss about how much I like to give presentations and I'd been working on some slick charts to illustrate our overall strategy and performance. Being the truly unselfish person that she is, my boss agreed to give me the chance to present at our annual meeting. All of which amounted to a great opportunity for me.

Except for one thing: I have this bad habit of thinking I have to be perfect at whatever I do. If everyone else isn't happy with my performance, somehow I've failed. It's a type-A thing, no doubt about it. I'm sure I learned it at some point way back in my misty past, and it has become one of those ingrained beliefs that I've had to "unlearn." When I am being rational, I know it's completely unrealistic. Nobody really cares that much if I make a mistake, as long as I'm willing to clean up the mess. People are much more interested in a genuine effort than a perfect effort. They would much rather have the real me than some over-rehearsed, sounds-like-he-memorized-it guy droning away through a set of immaculate charts.

But as I'm sure you know from your own experience, our bad habits can be incredibly difficult to overcome, especially in times of stress. For whatever reason, stress seems to feed bad habits, blowing them completely out of proportion into huge demons that practically chase us around the room. So there I was, the night before the presentation, telling myself I had to get some sleep, trying to force myself not to worry. Ever try to force yourself to relax? It doesn't work. The harder I tried the worse it got. I knew I was being ridiculous which made me mad at myself and that, in turn, only made it harder to sleep. I was tired, trying to make myself sleep, and with every passing moment getting madder at myself. Totally crazy. I ended up going the *entire night* without sleeping a wink. By the time dawn crept into the room, I was feeling like a washcloth wrung out by the incredible hulk. Rip roarin' and ready to collapse, that was me. Why worry? It only felt like my job was on the line.

However—and here's the key—I did the presentation anyway. I didn't have any energy left for worrying. All I could do was just go be myself and see what happened. So I walked in and *gave the presentation the way I wanted to, worry and all.* Can you see how that was a win worth celebrating? I was trying to break a bad habit—this ridiculous notion of having to be perfect—and the only way that was going to happen was if I did what I wanted to do despite the old feelings. When I look back on it, I realize I *needed* that sleepless night. It was important, maybe critically so, because it showed me that my old way of thinking didn't have to rule my future. If I was going to break through to a new way of thinking, I was going to have to do it with my old way of thinking still playing those old records in my head. The two ways of thinking, the old and the new, had to co-exist in my head for a while. I needed to experience the fact that the old thoughts could be there and I could still do what I wanted.

To me, that cork represents a huge win. It reminds me that nothing about my past has to drag me down. It's my own small win (ritual 4) and it became one of the foundations of a new confidence. It was concrete proof to me that I could create the life I wanted no matter what I had been taught to think. Every time I face down an old demon I think about that cork. I've done it many times now (with the corks to prove it) to the point where I now have my own long history of wins over my old ways of thinking that I no longer accept. When I travel now to give a presentation, I sleep like a baby. Same situation, completely different experience. All because I've created my own positive history—I've bootstrapped myself—and I've done it through a simple ritual of taking the time to give myself a pat on the back.

How did that presentation go on that sleepless morning? For me it was great. I'd let myself out of a box I'd been in for years. How did it go for everyone else? I don't know…you'd have to ask them.

Story: Who You Talkin' To, Coach?

I love mentoring other people. Besides the fact that it makes you feel great to help someone else, there is nothing like a coaching session to give you a good look in the mirror at your own behavior. I'm not exactly sure why this pattern always emerges with the people I mentor, but it probably has something to do with the fact that almost any topic I would mentor someone about is a topic I am facing myself. It probably also has something to do with the fact that the people I am attracted to mentoring in the first place, the ones I feel I can actually help, are people who share something in common with me. They are where I was yesterday and their struggles were my own. I can't help but see myself in their efforts.

For instance, there's the story of the guy I coach who wants to write. He's good at it, better than he believes. He's also worried about doing it "just right." I can't tell you how many times we have discussed how hard it is to find time to sit down and write when there is so much to be so busy about. I find myself telling him, "don't try to do everything all at once, just get something down on the page. Turn off the spell checker, turn off the grammar checker and just write. Don't worry about what comes out, you can edit that later. We're talking about developing a process; once you get writing on a regular basis the results will follow. Yeah I know it can be frightening to think about thousands of people reading your book and criticizing your work, but you have to run right at that kind of fear. The sooner you face it, the sooner you will find it's something you can get past." Ironically, it somehow always seems to work out that we will have a coaching session like this on one of those days where I've gone a whole week without making the time to write in my own book. How's that for the pot calling the kettle black?

Then there's the other guy I coach who is impatient. He wants everything to happen now, or preferably yesterday. He can't stand to see himself not making immediate progress. He wants to know the answer now, as though everything is a race he has to win. He may not be as type-A as I am, but it's a close call. We talk a lot about process. We talk a lot about celebrating the small wins along the way rather than worrying about the big win at the end. Sometimes I think the main purpose of our calls is for me to help him celebrate the progress he has made. In the space of two years, he has changed jobs, moved to a different part of the country, moved again to a location that cut his commute time, and convinced his management to pay for him to pursue a graduate degree in business so he can lay the foundation to switch careers. He's got so much going on that his busy meter is buried on max. We've been talking a lot recently about quiet time. I haven't convinced him yet that it is the key he is looking for, that the only way he's going to find what he wants is to slow down enough to hear it. But we're working on it. I find it interesting that I am having these discussions with him just at a time when I've loaded myself up with so many things to do that I've been missing out on my own quiet time. Anything significant there, do you think, or just coincidence?

Yeah, there's nothing like coaching for meeting yourself on the road to wherever it is you are going. It's like telling your kids "do what I say, not what I do!" It's always so much easier to see faults in someone else, to be the Monday morning quarterback. We love to criticize the athlete who "psyched himself out," but how many of us do any better when we are on the playing field? Coaching helps you bridge that gap. When you coach, you are talking to yourself. The difference is, you can't fool another person as easily as you can fool yourself. Force yourself to explain a concept to someone else, and you will understand it better yourself.

Story: On The Ropes

Think of a scene. You are watching a boxing match, say one of the Olympic matches. The U.S. boxer (or pick your own favorite nationality) is not doing well. He came out fighting but took a particularly hard blow that put him off his game. At this point, he's just trying to get to the end of the round. He's got his gloves up desperately trying to protect himself from another staggering punch. He's literally on the ropes, and it's all he can do just to keep his feet. He's not making progress, he's surviving.

Life ever feel that way to you? I remember having this experience as part of a job change. I'd switched jobs to another part of the company to do something that sounded great. It was a chance to get in on the ground floor of a brand new program, and the role I would be playing sounded like more fun than should be allowed. So I jumped on the offer when I got it. However, after about a month, I found myself completely tangled up in a bad habit of mine: I was being "Mr. Nice." You know how it goes in a new group. You are new, you want everybody to like you, and most of all you want to feel like you are making a contribution. That latter feeling can be overpowering, especially when it seems like everyone else knows what's going on and knows their place in the scheme of things. By contrast there you are, trying to make sense out of the acronyms everyone is throwing around, wanting to ask a million questions but not wanting to appear stupid. And so you are eager to volunteer, to prove your worth, and you jump at the chance to make a contribution. That's a trap, of course, because there is always a ton of detail work to go around.

Yet, there I was: I'd walked right into the trap, and had loaded myself up with work that had nothing directly to do with my job. Naturally, I found I was frustrated. Suddenly, I didn't like work anymore. But how could that be? It was such a cool job; only a few weeks before I was pinching myself because it all seemed too good to be true. How could I feel like work was a grind already? How could I have gotten on the ropes so quickly? Most importantly, how could I set things right?

The answer (and I'll bet you knew this was coming) is quiet time. Whenever I find myself "feeling reactive," the answer is always to seek out the quiet time to help me get back to being active.

What do I mean by "reactive?" I mean feelings like "I am doing everything for everyone else." I mean frenzied feelings, like "all I do is spend all day putting out fires." Of course, we always have some things we need to do for others; I'm not talking about that. I'm talking about when you feel like your entire day is spent where you feel like you are somebody else's slave, and you reach the end of the day feeling like you got nothing done that *you* wanted to get done. In this story, I had started a great job that I was excited about, but in my zeal to fit in, I was taking on everyone else's grunt work. I couldn't point to any goal *that I was pursuing*. I was just "doing stuff for everyone else." I felt like "a go-for," like an errand boy.

Quiet time is the perfect remedy for this problem. It hits it squarely between the eyes because it forces you to stop all the frenzy. And note that you don't have to have a major revolt to make this happen. One of the things I pride myself on is being able to keep my commitments. I had taken on all these "chores" and I felt like I wanted to honor those commitments. So I am not suggesting that you suddenly "go postal" at work, abdicate all responsibility, and shout "you know, none of this crap is what I'm supposed to be doing!" What I'm talking about is being disciplined about making sure that every day, without fail, you take a little "time out" to remember ask yourself what you want to do.

So that's what I did. I started taking a half hour each day at work, right at the top of the morning, to shut off all the electronic forms of communication and just think about my job. Why had I taken the job in the first place? What was it that had attracted me? What could I shoot for that would really get my juices flowing again? It didn't take long for me to remember what was "cool" about the job. In fact, it got to be fun. I got to where I was looking forward to my "morning meetings with myself" as I called them (I literally scheduled them on my calendar). The great thing about putting them at the top of my day was that they had a way of giving my entire day a focus. I'd end the meeting with a goal, as in "today, I'd really like to see if I can get such-and-such done." Having that goal made all the difference in the world. It gave form to my day. It made my day truly *my* day. All the other "chores" that I'd picked up were things to be fit in around the real point of my day. I kept those commitments, but also started working on the things I wanted to do. My attitude did a 180, and I was looking forward to work again.

I guess the other thing that stands out for me in this story is the fact that quiet time, and passions, don't always have to be about earth-shattering topics. I'm not talking about the need to completely reinvent yourself, although I'm convinced quiet time helps with that too. I'm suggesting that quiet time can be most powerfully used as a habit, to keep ourselves on track. Yes, taking 40 days and 40 nights off to contemplate the meaning of life would be wonderful. If you have that kind of time, good for you. Go for it. But even taking 30 minutes a day each morning just to remind yourself of what is important in your life *can* make a huge difference. My own belief is that I get more out of the regular habit of quiet time than I would out of a once-in-a-lifetime two month sabbatical. A once-in-a-lifetime experience is just that: something I experience once. A habit is more like a good friend that will stick by me through think and thin.

The quiet time in this story paid me back in spades because it gave me something concrete. It gave me a process I could use to ensure I didn't lose myself in all the frenzy. It continues to be one of the most powerful techniques I have in my toolbox for getting "back on track" when I start to feel frustrated.

Give it a try. In fact, give all these rituals a try. Take some quiet time each day. Run straight at your fears when they arise so you can get them behind you as quickly as possible. Celebrate your small wins—you've earned them. And reinforce it all by coaching someone else. I promise you that if you do these things, you will give yourself the structure you need to make your work-life balancing commitments stick.

5   Be "Selfirst"

Principle 5: Put yourself first. Most of us are taught that looking after our own needs is selfish and we overcompensate by completely ignoring our needs. The busier you get in life, the more important it becomes to make sure you are taking care of yourself.

Put YOUR Mask On First

"...Should we experience a sudden change in cabin pressure, an oxygen mask will automatically deploy from the compartment above your seat. Reach up, grasp your mask, and pull firmly to start the flow of oxygen. Place the mask over your nose and mouth and tighten the adjustable straps on either side of the mask. If you are seated next to someone who needs assistance with their mask, *put your mask on first* and then help the person next to you..."

Anyone who has flown on an airplane has heard something like the above. It's part of the pre-take-off ritual of any commercial airline flight. Like most travelers, I'm getting to the point where I've heard this so many times I don't even listen to the words any more. I can recite them by heart; in fact, I did just that when I sat down to write this chapter.

How curious, then, that this snippet of airplane etiquette which goes largely ignored should hold the secret to the *most important* principle of work-life balancing I could possibly share with you. How interesting that so many of us have memorized something that holds the key to keeping our lives balanced and happy, and yet fail to heed the advice.

Put your mask on first. Consider why they tell us this. Imagine, for a moment (though probably nobody wants to) that you are on an airplane which suffers a "sudden change in cabin pressure." I've never had the experience and, God willing, I never will. But I can imagine what it would be like. First would come surprise, perhaps laced with a bit of annoyance. "What the Hell is going on?" and "damn it, I just spilled Coke all over my pants!" would be followed swiftly by "holy shit!" and shortly thereafter by complete pandemonium. I imagine myself sitting next to my 5-year-old daughter who looks at me with all that trust in her eyes and still thinks of her Daddy as infallible, and my one overwhelming desire would be to make sure she was OK. She's just so precious to me, I can't imagine not wanting to do everything in my power to help her. And like most men, I want to feel like I am doing something useful in a crisis, not just sitting around waiting for the next shoe to fall.

But notice what do they tell us to do *first:* "put *your* mask on *first.*" I'm guessing here that the phrase "sudden change in cabin pressure" is probably a euphemism for something more descriptive like "listen up, bone head: when the you-know-what hits the fan you've got exactly 30 seconds to get that mask on your chops if you don't want to pass out." I have no idea how much time there is, of course, and I'm sure the military has had plenty of experience with fighter pilots to know just exactly how much time there really is and it has all been built into the system with plenty of tolerance to spare. And of course, even if you did pass out, there is still a window of time where someone else can get your mask on for you and you would be fine. But then, it would be up to someone else to do that for you. Either way, a sudden change in cabin pressure can't leave loads of free time. Most importantly, if you want to be effective, if you want to know you have done something useful with yourself in the situation, you need to act with purpose, without doubt, and you need to act by taking care of yourself first.

It's a great analogy to work-life balancing. When I was younger, work-life balancing was not much of an issue. But then, I had a mother and father to take care of most of the really tough stuff like food, shelter, clothing, and dealing with pesky telemarketers. There was so little "cabin pressure" that there really was no threat. I had plenty of time to "get my mask on" when I needed the extra air. It wasn't until I got older and took on my own set of responsibilities that the "pressure went up" in my "cabin." Like almost anyone reading this book, I now find I have plenty of pressure (more than enough, thank you very much) and lots of commitments on top of it to boot. People depend upon me and I feel an obligation to keep my commitments. It's as though I'm flying the plane and I have passengers on board for whom I feel responsible.

For some "sudden changes in cabin pressure" I do, in fact, do the right thing. All of us do—you see it all the time. Someone at work suffers a family loss (say, the death of a parent) and they drop everything to take care of themselves and their family. A co-worker will have a heart attack or some other bout with a serious disease—a sudden change in pressure, if you will—and they will immediately take a time out for themselves. Nobody balks at such behavior. We all understand; in fact, the universal reaction is something like "hey, I completely understand. Just let me know what I can do to help."

But what if the change in cabin pressure is not so sudden? What if, by contrast, it's a slow leak? What if, instead of some dramatic event that captures your attention, like the death of a family member, you experience a lot of small events which seem insignificant by themselves. What if you experience "pressure creep" like a slow, piling-on of more and more demands until you suddenly find, to your surprise, that all the oxygen has been sucked out of your "cabin?" What if you knew the cabin had a slow leak and you started racing down the aisle, trying to make sure everybody on your plane had their masks on, only to find that before you could take care of everyone else, your time had run out and you were flat on your face in the back of the plane, without a mask, wondering what the heck went wrong?

I think that's what happens to most of us. I think we gradually do more and more for everyone else, and less and less for ourselves, until one day we suddenly realize there's been a change in "cabin pressure" but we can't remember how it happened. We get so busy taking care of everybody else and every other commitment in our lives that we don't ever take the time to address our own needs. We end up at the back of the airplane, completely worn out, gasping for breath, confused and angry because we feel like we've been doing everything we were "supposed" to do and we still ended up feeling like the plane is going down.

Being "Selfirst"

So you have to put yourself first, and not just when there is a dramatic event. After all, what's the point of waiting until you have a heart attack to take care of your health? You have to make a habit of keeping up with your needs because nobody else is going to do it. And you have to get over feeling guilty about it, because it's not just you that suffers when you suffer. Everyone who depends upon you suffers too. You can't be any good for anyone else if you run yourself into the ground. You need to be what I call "selfirst."

Notice that I have made up a new word here. That wasn't a gimmick; I found I had no choice. As I got thinking about how to write this chapter I naturally started to think of ways to describe the concept of "putting yourself first in a positive way." But I ran into a problem I have never faced before. I ran out of words, and for a guy who's not bashful about talking that's saying something. As far as I can tell, we don't have a word in our language to describe this concept. We have some words and phrases that come close, but they are all negative in one way or another. Isn't that interesting? I think that says something very profound about our culture. Think about it: we have no single word that we can use to describe how it's possible to be doing something for yourself without that being negative.

Take the word "selfish" for instance. It definitely has a negative connotation. How many of us as parents have told our kids not to be selfish? "You'd better share your toys with your brother. If you're selfish, nobody will want to play with you." So "selfish" is out because it's too negative. OK, then what about "self-oriented?" Well that's a bit better; it doesn't have quite the negative doing-it-at-the-expense-of-somebody-else meaning that "selfish" has. But "self-oriented" is too shallow. It's used to describe someone who is so obsessed with themselves that they don't even think about anyone else. They may not be actively denying others for their own gain (that would selfish), but they certainly aren't thinking of anyone but themselves either.

What's left? Self-sufficient? That sounds like somebody who can survive in the forest with nothing but some tooth picks and a nail file. Self-centered? Nope, that's the same as "stuck up." Self-actualized? I'm not even sure exactly what that means except that it sounds vaguely diagnostic, like something you have to take a pill for. No, try as I might, I could find no word to describe what I wanted to say. And that's a crying shame, because it says we have a culture that has placed absolutely no emphasis at all on taking care of oneself. It's as though taking care of our own needs is so far down the list of acceptable activities that *we haven't even bothered to invent a word for it.*

We celebrate our ancestors who sacrificed to give their children a better life. We celebrate our heroes who made the ultimate sacrifice of giving their lives for their country. We create whole industries around how to sacrifice our hard-earned money to make our children happy. We excel at celebrating sacrifice; in fact, most of us celebrate sacrifice once a week every Sunday. But what about celebrating ourselves? What about celebrating those who maintain their ability to be peak performers in everything they do? What about honoring those who take the time and make the effort to keep themselves well-rested, happy, and healthy so they can maximize their impact as parents, employees and citizens? Doesn't that matter at all?

I say it does. In fact, I say it's the most positive thing you can do. Yes of course we all need to avoid being selfish. That goes without saying. Or maybe it does need saying and maybe it does need repeating so we don't just give in to pure gluttony. But just as it is destructive to be selfish, it is equally destructive to ignore our needs. What good is an employee who is so tired his attention span is cut in half? Do you think your boss would rather have 50% of a 60-hour week or 100% of a 45-hour week? Who wants a husband that works so much he never takes the time for romance? Who wants a father who is so tired he gets angry at the drop of a hat and never seems to have any spare time to volunteer for activities that involve his children? What are we men anyway? Are we people, or are we just walking wallets?

Not convinced yet? Sound a little bit too idealistic? I've run this by a lot of close friends and I can see it in their eyes; they want to believe what I am saying but just can't quite bring themselves around to my way of thinking. I have a reputation for being idealistic, and while my friends like that about me I often get the feeling they think all this nonsense about being selfirst is really just my way of looking at the world through my overly-rose-colored glasses. "That might work for you, Paul, but not for the rest of us."

Let me try one more argument for anyone who is still a hold-out. Let me draw a contrast between two ways of living through a single day—a "Tale of Two Days" as it were. Let's call them the "old day" and the "new day," and in both cases let's say that you have something you want to be doing that is extra curricular in some way. It might be working out, it might be starting your own business, it might be some new hobby that you are taking up. It doesn't matter; you know what it is for you. It is something you have always wanted to do *for you.*

Now, you have two different ways you can approach doing this thing for yourself, thus the "two days" in this tale. The first approach, the "old day," is the way you would probably approach doing things. You'd say to yourself, "self...I really want to do this new thing. In fact, by George, come Hell or high water I'm going to do it! But of course, I have obligations to meet, and I learned (like a good boy) that it's bad to be selfish. So I'm going to make sure I get everything done for everyone else first, and then I'll have the rest of the day to focus on my thing." And that sounds completely rational, right? That way, nobody can accuse you of being selfish or of shirking your responsibilities. So off to work you go (high ho!) all revved up about getting things done as quickly as possible so you can get to what you really want. Make the sacrifice first, then you get the reward. Dessert always comes last, right?

But the day wears on and you inevitably run into snags. Someone doesn't move as quickly as you'd like on something and it slows you down. You get frustrated with them, maybe even downright annoyed if they disagree with you or want to debate your approach. You find yourself frustrated, driving behind that person who wants to drive 55 in the left lane. What is their problem? Do they want to live their life on the road? Some of us have places to go, damn it! You manage to get through the work day and come home, a bit more tired than you'd like because you had to deal with all the morons at work that were too thick to see that doing things your way would have been far more efficient. It took extra energy to sort them out. And now, your kids want to goof around, and your wife wants to talk about her day, and it's not that you really mind all that but…well…it's just been a long day and you have been looking forward to devoting some time for yourself. I mean, damn it, you put in all this effort for everyone else—can't they see you just want a little time for yourself? Is that asking too much?

Do you see how backwards this is? It's as if you've been spending the whole day like it was the last day of school before summer vacation. All you wanted was to hear the bell ring so you could dash out of school and start having fun. You weren't paying any attention in class, and the clock seemed to have stopped moving. All you have been thinking about is that one thing you really want to get done for yourself today. You can't wait for the day to be over so you can finally give yourself the treat you've been looking forward to. In fact, that may say it all in a nutshell—you spent your day "looking forward."

By contrast, imagine you did things differently. In our second approach, the "new day," you make sure that the *very first thing you do* is take some time to make progress on the thing you really want to do. You put it right up front. Right out of bed, maybe even before you take a shower or before anyone else gets up, you are downstairs doing your hobby, or you've headed off to the gym for a pre-dawn workout, or whatever. The point is, *you get your stuff done first.* Of course, you probably have to set a timer to remind yourself to quit after some reasonable period of time because otherwise you'll get to having so much fun the entire day will get away from you. But you make sure you get something done for yourself first.

How do you think the rest of the day goes now? I can guaranty you that it's far easier and far more pleasant. You aren't "looking forward," you're not living your day in the future, because you've already accomplished something for

171

yourself. You are happy, proud of yourself for getting something done you have always wanted to do, and that makes you much more content. You can live in the present instead of the future. When you get to work you are 100% "at work" versus having your mind wandering off to something else. And when you get home, perhaps still tired out from a long day, you are happy to let your hair down and play with the kids or just sit and listen to your spouse. Your day is done, and you've already done something special for yourself. You can enjoy the "main course" without worrying about saving room for dessert because you've already had dessert. You made sure you had it first.

Now you tell me which you prefer: the "old day" or the "new day?" Which day is the most productive overall? Which day puts you in the better frame of mind for keeping the commitments you've made? And last, but by no means least, which day ensures you are getting something done for yourself?

Being "selfirst" means being committed to living the most positive, productive life you can. It means having the courage to take time for yourself, so you can be a more complete person for those around you. It means setting an example of how to live a full, balanced life so that those you influence will be inspired to do the same. Above all, it means recognizing that *peak performance in life flows directly from your ability to take care of yourself.* You can't have one without the other. If you want to be a good dad, a good husband, a good friend, or a good employee, you have to be a good "you" first.

172

Story: The Last Story

If you hear a note of frustration coming through in this story, that is intended. The timing here was ironic, because it occurred precisely as I was writing this chapter. I got myself so tangled up, that the only way out was by being selfirst...but I'm getting ahead of myself. Let me start at the beginning.

So there I was writing this book on work-life balancing. In fact, I was writing the discussion of how to be selfirst and why that is so important. Seems like I have it all figured out, right? No reason why I should ever slip back into an unbalanced lifestyle, right? Ha! The reality is that it happens to us all. We figure out what we want to do and set up plans to get things moving forward. Everything seems to be on track. And then there comes a day when we wake up one morning with an inexplicable feeling of frustration. For me, it's a tension below my neck, right between the shoulder blades, that sort of lodges itself there. About two weeks ago I found myself waking up in the morning with this little knot in my back and, of course, feeling frustrated. At the time, I hadn't a clue as to why.

I was near the end of writing this book, and had somehow managed to go a whole month without writing a thing. There was just "too much to do"—too many emails to answer, too many kids activities to attend, too many "critical" tasks at work. I was staying up late, getting up early, doing what felt like a ton of work. You know the drill: you feel like you get up at 5:30 a.m. and work until 11:00 p.m. and there isn't a spare moment in your day. You even eat at your desk.

How frustrating it is, then, to be working so hard and yet feeling like nothing is getting done. I felt like I was working myself to the nub, like I could see the new wrinkles popping out in the mirror each morning, like every time I blinked my hairline receded just a bit more. And yet, all that seemed to be happening was that more work was piling up. And it wasn't like I could point to an excuse. It would have been one thing if I could have said "yeah, work is piling up, but that's because I've been taking extra time to write my book." Unfortunately, that wasn't the case; all I was doing was work and I was still falling behind. So not only was I not making any progress, but I didn't even have anything to show for it! I was working my butt off and going backwards. It was doing so much of everything that nothing was getting done. I was "a mile wide and an inch deep" as the saying goes, and every inch of progress I'd make in one area would be erased the next day as two more inches would pile up. It was like I was trying to shovel snow for the whole neighborhood, and I could manage to get an inch removed from everyone's driveway each day, but two more inches would fall every night.

I looked at my wife one night as we dragged ourselves up to bed and told her I was ready to just quit. We joked about it for a bit, fantasizing (as we often do) about just taking the credit cards, jumping in the car with a wild sort of giggle on our lips, and seeing how long we can go before someone makes us stop. We had worked so hard to have "everything" we had used up all our energy in the process. What's the point of "having it all" if you can't enjoy any of "it?" It's like multiplying by zero; no matter how large a number is, if you multiply by zero you end up with nothing.

That's when my wife made an off-hand remark that hit me like a brick. She said "you know, I'm just so tired I can't even think straight. If I could ever just slow down enough to catch my breath, I might be able to sort this out."

Ding!

So I said, rather excitedly, "Kath...you just gave me an idea for a new 'project' for us!" OK, I admit it; not the best timing. When your wife is dead tired is not the best time to suggest a new project. She gave me that glare every guy knows so well...the one that says "you are on thin ice, mister!" The last thing she wanted to hear was a new project after she'd just told me she was so tired she was ready to chuck it all. But as I described my idea she warmed to it. Why not make getting our rest our most important project? Dishes still in the sink? Leave 'em, it's time for bed. Taxes still due? Blow it off and we'll file for an extension, it's time for bed. Birthday presents to buy? Toys to put away? Finances to rebalance? Clothes to be cleaned? Shopping to be done? Some name-your-favorite-deadline-issue just burning to be addressed? Ignore it all...our first priority, our "main project," would be getting our sleep. And we'd make a commitment: for one month we'd be utterly committed to making sure that no matter what else was going on, we would get our rest. We would be selfirst.

The difference was amazing. Even after only a week, I felt like a new person. I had more energy in the morning. I stopped falling asleep after lunch. I suddenly found time to start writing again...this story, in fact, was the first thing out of hopper. I made more progress at work because I felt like it was easier to focus. And that knot in my back even loosened; I was making progress again and I could see the results.

It's been almost a month now and I have done more work in that month than during the previous month which was so frustrating, even though I'm taking more time out to get my sleep, and I'm taking more time to write. I even feel like I'm getting to spend more time with my wife and kids. It's completely backwards from what you would expect; by spending *less* time working I am getting *more* work done. And it's all because I show up for work with a full tank, versus trying to drive on fumes. In fact, I show up with a full tank, as it were, for everything that I do; home, work, wife, kids, friends, whatever. There is more of "me" to go around because there is more of "me" in the first place. I'm happy and content because I know I am getting things done for myself that really matter to me. In short, everything else in my life has benefited from the fact that I am making a point to take care of myself first. I can't tell you how many times this story has played itself out for me. It comes in various forms and it happens in various contexts, but the result it always the same: I get more done for *other people* by making sure I *focus on myself first*.

I'm anxiously awaiting the end of this story. What will things be like in a month? How will Kathryn's life change and how will that affect me? Will we find ourselves arguing less often? Will we find ourselves having more fun? Will we see younger, happier faces in the mirror? Will we have an evening conversation that goes something like "you know, I really feel great about how things are going?" Most importantly, *will we stick to this habit of making sure we put ourselves first*?

I hope so. Because that's the whole point of this book, after all. It is, in fact, why I chose to move this chapter to the end of my book, rather than the beginning where you might argue is its more logical resting place. If you take only one thing away from what I have related, it should be to remember to be selfirst. When everything else fails, when you are the most depressed or down or feeling the most unbalanced, taking a selfirst time out is the best single action you can take to getting yourself back on course.

And that is what matters the most about this effort to me. When the dust settles, what matters is that you, the reader, have found a way to make your life better. For myself, perhaps the moral of the story is that I should carry around my own copy of this book and dog-ear this page...for those times when I forget to remember that balance is a story told from the inside out, and that the best way to keep our commitments to everyone else, the best way to keep our balance, is to keep our commitments to ourselves first.

Work-Life Balancing Quick Reference

One of the things I always want after I read a good how-to book is a "CliffsNotes" version that puts it all together in a compact form. I enjoy the read, but once I'm done I often want to review the key points without having to reread the full explanation. An index doesn't do it for me because it's too scattered. What I need is a good outline, with more meat on it than the table of contents, but with less text than the original.

What I've done here is combine the idea of a CliffsNotes with page references like you would find in an index. That way, you can come back here to refresh your memory on the main points, and if you need to jump back to the text for more explanation, or if you just want to reread a story that brings one of the principles to life, all the page references are here for you.

Principle 1: Be Process-Oriented (pg 23)

Make a fundamental paradigm shift to being process oriented versus outcome obsessed. Most of us interpret a desire to be "goal oriented" to mean the end result is everything. That is a mistake. Results are important, but you must focus on the process, not the end-game, and let the results come to you.

- Big results come from small, consistent process (see story *Little Drops of Water, Little Grains of Sand*, pg 30)

- If you really want to hit a milestone, focus on the process that best supports achieving that milestone. It gets you there the fastest (see story *Nobody Ever Hit a Milestone By Focusing On It*, pg 37)

- If you don't know exactly where you are going, you can still get to the right end result by simply picking a direction and getting started. If you stick with a good process, you will still get to the right goal even if you make a false start (see story *Making Progress by Going the Wrong Way*, pg 33)

Principle 2: Live Blame-Free (pg 41)

Principle 2: Commit to living your life completely without "blame." Do this by taking the phrase "I can't" out of you vocabulary and substituting "I want" instead. This will give you a powerful tool for breaking out of the beliefs that are holding you back.

- We all learn a destructive three-part belief system that teaches us to be externally focused (see pg 41), to rigidly follow the rules and standards set by others (see pg 42), and to avoid asking for help (see pg 46)

- Our default belief system leads to a "culture of blame," but you can turn the tables by using the same three-part belief system to drive yourself to a better life:

  - Play the "blame game" and take a blame inventory (see pg 50)

  - Use blame to determine what's important in your life (see pg 51)

180

- Then, go after what you want using the same three-part belief system:

  - Knowing your goal, and reality, use your energy to invent your own rules of the game (see pg 56)

  - Grade yourself (internally) by how well you stay focused on the process for getting to your goal (see pg 55)

  - Draw on your self-reliance to stick to your guns, knowing that you will become an inspiration to those around you (see pg 57)

  - As you need to, reinforce your actions with rituals (see Chapter 4, pg 107)

- Getting rid of blame will give you a huge boost in productivity (see story *With the Right Shades*, pg 60)

- Getting rid of blame will help you see obvious solutions that were "hidden" from you. You will be able to live differently and feel right about it (see story *The Parent Nanny*, pg 64; see story *Mom's Week Off*, pg 92; see story *Buck The System, Make Friends*, pg 146)

- When you get mired in blame, knowing you are holding yourself back but unable to identify the barriers, consider using the "walk through" ritual to break the log jam (see pg 127)

Principle 3: Embrace Your Passions (pg 73)

Principle 3: Find your passions in life and embrace them with every fiber of your being. If you do this, everything about your life will be easier, come faster, be healthier, take less time, and produce vastly more results. Nothing—absolutely nothing—can compete with passion.

- Passion will make your whole life more efficient. This will happen in several key ways:

  - A passion focus will reduce life's overhead (see pg 74, see story *Less Time, More results*, pg 94)

  - Passion leads to faster decision making (see pg 78)

  - Passion allows you to live without doubt (see pg 79)

  - Being focused on your passion will automatically create new opportunities for you (see pg 82; see story *The Opportunity Escalator*, pg 99)

- If you endorse a process of following your passions, you will find this process is identical to the work-life balancing process (see pg 84; see story *Always On--Curse or Opportunity?*, pg 89; see story *Mom's Week Off*, pg 92)

- Others will judge you more positively if you are following your passion (see story *A Tale of Two Employees*, pg 87)

- Suggestions on how to find your passion (see pg 105; see "Ritual 1: Get Quiet, Hear Your Passion," pg 112)

Principle 4: Reinforce With Rituals (pg 107)

Principle 4: Make the time to build regular reinforcement rituals into your schedule. You will need these to keep your balance. Very few of us pay attention to regular maintenance activities because their repetitive nature can lull us into thinking they amount to wasted time. They do

not. They may not be glamorous, but they are essential—
you will fail without them.

• Living a balanced life will feel wrong, because our
culture doesn't promote balance (see pg 108; see story
Sticking Out and The Spare Tire, pg 143)

• Bucking the system does not mean you have to create
havoc. Most people will want to help you in your
balancing efforts (see story *Buck The System, Make
Friends*, pg 146)

• Rituals are the key to getting back on track, and there
are four key rituals you should follow:

   • Use quiet time to reset your priorities (see pg 112;
   see story *On The Ropes*, pg 159)

   • To get past the fears that are holding you back, the
   most effective thing you can do is run straight at
   them (see pg 117; see story *Run for the Border*,
   pg 151)

   • Coaching others on work-life balancing will be a
   huge boost to your own efforts at keeping balanced
   (see pg 120; see story *Who You Talkin' To, Coach?*,
   pg 157)

   • Make sure you celebrate small "victories" to build
   up your own history of success. That will give you
   a sense of pride in yourself that you can draw on to
   keep yourself going (see pg 125; see story
   Celebrating a Sleepless Night, pg 154)

• There are two other rituals I recommend you use on an
as-needed basis (versus the previous four rituals which
should be practiced regularly):

- Use the "walk through" technique to unmask deeply held beliefs that are holding you back (see pg 127; see story *The Parent Nanny*, pg 64)

- Use the "Rule of Judgment" to help you during those times when peer pressure is at its worst (see pg 134; see story *Sticking Out and The Spare Tire*, pg 143)

Principle 5: Be "Selfirst" (pg 163)

Principle 5: Put yourself first. Most of us are taught that looking after our own needs is selfish and we over-compensate by completely ignoring our needs. The busier you get in life, the more important it becomes to make sure you are taking care of yourself.

- You must take care of yourself if you are to have any hope of having a balanced life (see pg 163)

- It is difficult to put yourself first in a positive way because we are never taught how. In fact, our language has no word for the concept (see pg 167)

- Putting yourself first is the most productive thing you can do—for yourself and for everyone else (see story *The Last Story*, pg 173)

About the Author

Paul Baffes, Ph.D., a work-life balance coach and speaker who has helped thousands world wide to address their work-life balance needs. He is the father of 2, with a full-time working spouse, and spends much of his free time experimenting with new ways of demonstrating the value of balance to everything from individual happiness to corporate productivity.

For information regarding individual coaching, speaking engagements, or work-life balance training and seminars, please email us at contact@drworklife.com or write to Paul Baffes, 8127 Mesa Drive, Suite B206-262, Austin, Texas, 78759.